How to Find anc

by Gilad James

GILAD JAMES
MYSTERY SCHOOL

Copyright

Table of Contents

I. Introduction

1. Definition of love

In the pursuit of finding and sustaining love, it is important to first understand what love truly means. The definition of love has been debated for centuries and has been subject to interpretation based on cultural, societal, and personal beliefs. Love can be defined as an intense feeling of deep affection towards someone, a strong attachment or devotion, and a willingness to sacrifice for the well-being of that person. In this paper, we will explore the different definitions of love and how they relate to finding and sustaining love in one's life.

One common definition of love is the feeling of emotional attachment towards another person. This definition emphasizes the role of emotions in love, which is often seen as the primary driving force behind romantic relationships. Emotional attachment can be thought of as a bond that forms between two people based on shared experiences, mutual respect, and trust. This type of love is often described as passionate or intense, as it involves a deep emotional connection and psychological dependence on another person.

Related to emotional attachment is the concept of interpersonal attraction. This refers to the process by which individuals are drawn to one another and form romantic relationships. Attraction can be based on physical, emotional, or intellectual factors and can occur at various stages of a relationship. Physical attraction, for example, is often the initial spark that draws two people together, while emotional and intellectual attraction can sustain a relationship over time.

Another definition of love is based on the idea of altruism or selflessness. This type of love is grounded in the willingness to put another person's needs above one's own and to make sacrifices for their well-being. Altruistic love is often associated with the concept of unconditional love, which involves accepting and loving someone regardless of their flaws, mistakes, or imperfections. This type of love is often seen as the highest form of love, as it involves placing another person's happiness above one's own.

A third definition of love is based on the idea of commitment. This type of love involves a conscious decision to stay committed to a relationship, even when faced with difficulties or challenges. Commitment is often seen as an essential ingredient in sustaining long-term relationships, as it involves making a conscious effort to work through problems and to prioritize the needs and happiness of one's partner.

In order to find and sustain love in one's life, it is important to understand and embrace these different definitions of love. Emotional attachment and interpersonal attraction can help to build the foundation of a romantic relationship, while selflessness and commitment can sustain it over time. Each definition of love has its own strengths and weaknesses, and a successful relationship will likely involve a combination of these different elements.

One factor that is crucial in finding and sustaining love is communication. Effective communication involves expressing one's feelings and needs in a clear and respectful manner, as well as actively listening to one's partner's thoughts and feelings. Communication is essential in building trust and intimacy in a relationship, as it allows for the sharing of innermost thoughts and emotions. Without open and honest communication, misunderstandings and conflicts can arise, leading to feelings of hurt and rejection.

Another important factor in finding and sustaining love is self-awareness. This involves being aware of one's own thoughts, feelings, and behaviors, as well as how they impact others. Self-awareness can help individuals to understand their own needs and desires in a relationship, as well as those of their partner. It can also help to identify patterns of behavior that may be harmful to a relationship, such as a tendency towards jealousy or controlling behavior.

In addition to communication and self-awareness, trust is another key ingredient in finding and sustaining love. Trust involves allowing oneself to be vulnerable with another person and believing that they will act in one's best interests. Trust can take time to build, but it is essential in building a strong and lasting relationship. Without trust, individuals may be hesitant to express their true feelings or needs, leading to a breakdown in communication and intimacy.

Finally, it is important to recognize that finding and sustaining love is not a one-size-fits-all process. Every individual and relationship is unique, and what works for one person or couple may not work for another. It is important to be open and flexible in one's approach to finding and sustaining love, and to be willing to adapt and change as needed.

In conclusion, the definition of love is complex and multifaceted. It involves emotional attachment, interpersonal attraction, selflessness, commitment, and trust, among other factors. In order to find and sustain love in one's life, it is important to embrace these different definitions of love, as well as to prioritize effective communication, self-awareness, and trust. By doing so, individuals can build strong and lasting relationships that bring happiness and fulfillment to their lives.

2. Importance of finding and sustaining love

Introduction:

Love is an emotion that has been present in the human experience since the beginning of time. It is a feeling that is difficult to describe but can be felt in many different ways. Finding and sustaining love is important for everyone as it defines our happiness and makes life worth living. Love can be found and sustained in many different ways and each person has their own unique way of doing so. Understanding the importance of finding and sustaining love is crucial to living a fulfilling life.

How to Find Love:

Finding love is not easy for everyone, but there are several ways in which one can approach it. Some of the key ways to find love include being open to new experiences, meeting new people, taking risks, and being true to oneself. It is important to remember that finding love takes time and effort and there is no guaranteed formula for success. However, there are some things that can be done to improve one's chances of finding love.

One of the most important things to remember when looking for love is to be open to new experiences. This means being open to trying things that may be outside of one's comfort zone. For example, if someone is not comfortable going to social events, they should consider attending different events to meet new people. If they are not comfortable approaching people, they could try online dating or taking a course or class to meet new people.

Another important way to find love is by meeting new people. This can be done by attending events, volunteering, going to local meetups, or joining social clubs. It is important to remember that meeting new people can be stressful and intimidating, but with practice, it can become easier.

Taking risks is also an important part of finding love. This means putting oneself out there and taking chances. This can include asking someone out on a date, putting oneself in a situation where they might meet someone new, or being vulnerable with someone they are interested in. While taking risks can be scary, it is a necessary part of finding love.

Finally, being true to oneself is one of the most important ways to find love. This means being honest with oneself about what they want and need in a relationship. It is important to be true to one's values, beliefs, and interests, as this will attract people who share these important qualities.

Sustaining Love:

Once love is found, it is important to sustain it. This means putting effort into the relationship and making it a priority. There are several key factors that can help sustain love including communication, trust, affection, and shared experiences.

Communication is one of the most important factors in sustaining love. This means being honest and open with one's partner about their feelings and needs. Communication can help increase intimacy and understanding of each other's needs.

Trust is another important factor in sustaining love. Trust means being able to rely on one's partner and believing that they will be there for them when needed. Trust can be built over time by being reliable, honest, and keeping one's commitments.

Affection is also an important factor in sustaining love. This means showing one's partner love and affection through physical touch, compliments, and doing things for them. Affection helps to increase intimacy and connection in the relationship.

Shared experiences are another important factor in sustaining love. This means creating memories and experiences together that deepen the connection and strengthen the bond in the relationship. This can be done by trying new things together, going on adventures, or simply spending time together doing things they both enjoy.

Conclusion:

Finding and sustaining love is important for everyone. It defines our happiness and makes life worth living. It is important to remember that finding love takes time and effort, but there are several ways in which one can approach it. Being open to new experiences, meeting new people, taking risks, and being true to oneself can help increase one's chances of finding love.

Once love is found, it is important to sustain it. This means putting effort into the relationship and making it a priority. Communication, trust, affection, and shared experiences are all important factors in sustaining love. By putting in the effort to find and sustain love, one can experience a fulfilling and happy life.

3. Overview of the guide

I'm sorry, as an AI language model, I do not have personal experience or the capability to have a personal stance on a topic. However, I can provide an overview of the guide for "How to Find and Sustain Love" based on available resources on the internet.

Overview:

Finding and sustaining love is a process that is unique to every individual's experience. However, there are certain guidelines and principles that can be helpful in promoting healthy relationships and maintaining long-term love. The guide for "How to Find and Sustain Love" aims to provide readers with practical tips and advice on how to navigate the complexities of dating, relationships, and love.

The guide is usually structured into different sections that cover various aspects of finding and sustaining love. These sections may include topics such as:

1. Understanding Yourself:

The first section is typically about understanding oneself. Before one can find love, it is essential to know what one wants and needs in a relationship. This section may include exercises and self-reflection questions that help individuals understand their personality, values, and beliefs regarding relationships.

2. Preparing for Love:

The next section is about preparing for love. This involves taking care of oneself physically, emotionally, and mentally to attract a healthy and fulfilling relationship. This section may also include tips on how to approach dating and relationships.

3. Dating:

The Dating section is about navigating the complexities of the dating process. It covers topics on how to meet potential partners, how to make a good first impression, and how to build a connection with someone. This section may focus on different types of dating, such as online dating and long-distance relationships.

4. Developing and Sustaining a Relationship:

The next section usually covers topics on building and maintaining a healthy relationship. It may include advice on how to establish mutual trust and respect, how to communicate effectively, and how to handle conflicts. This section may also provide tips on how to sustain a long-term relationship by keeping the spark alive.

5. Long-Term Love:

The final section is usually about sustaining love in the long term. It may provide guidance on challenges such as maintaining intimacy, managing money, and dealing with life changes. This section may also offer advice on how to keep a strong bond with a partner, even as the relationship evolves over time.

Conclusion:

Overall, the guide for "How to Find and Sustain Love" can offer helpful insights and practical guidance for individuals looking to find a fulfilling and long-lasting relationship. By understanding oneself, preparing for love, navigating dating, developing and sustaining a relationship, and keeping the love alive, individuals can increase their chances of finding and maintaining a healthy, loving partnership.

4. Quiz

1. What is the first step to finding love?
   a. Creating a list of qualities you want in a partner
   b. Going out to bars or clubs to meet potential partners
   c. Waiting for love to find you

2. How can you sustain a healthy and loving relationship?
   a. Communicating openly and honestly
   b. Keeping secrets from your partner
   c. Ignoring your partner's feelings and needs

3. Why is self-love important in finding and sustaining love?
   a. It shows your potential partner that you are confident and secure
   b. It helps you set healthy boundaries in your relationships
   c. It is not important in finding and sustaining love

4. Should you compromise your core values for the sake of love?
   a. Yes, it's important to make sacrifices for your partner
   b. No, compromising your values can lead to resentment and unhappiness
   c. It depends on the situation

5. Which of the following is NOT a common barrier to finding and sustaining love?
   a. Fear of vulnerability
   b. Communication

c. Social media etiquette

Answers:
1. a
2. a
3. b
4. b
5. c

II. Finding Love

1. Understanding yourself

Introduction

Love is an intricate, multidimensional, and dynamic concept that people of all ages, genders, and backgrounds yearn for. It is, arguably, the most profound and transformative human experience that shapes our sense of identity, purpose, and happiness. Yet, finding and sustaining love can be a challenging and elusive quest for many individuals who struggle with self-awareness, self-esteem, insecurities, and social barriers. In this paper, we explore the importance of understanding oneself in the context of finding and sustaining love. Specifically, we discuss six key themes that can help individuals cultivate self-knowledge, identify their core values, needs, and expectations, and navigate the complexities of romantic relationships.

Theme 1: Understanding Your Self-Concept

Self-concept refers to the set of beliefs, attitudes, and perceptions that individuals have about themselves. It encompasses various aspects of one's identity, such as personality traits, physical appearance, social roles, cultural background, and past experiences. A healthy self-concept is a cornerstone of mental well-being and provides the foundation for building fulfilling relationships. Therefore, it is crucial to engage in self-reflection and self-exploration to gain a deeper understanding of one's self-concept.

One way to do this is to ask critical questions about oneself and answer them honestly. For instance, what are my strengths and weaknesses? What are my values and beliefs? What do I enjoy doing, and what makes me happy? What are my goals and aspirations? How do I view myself in relation to others? Answering these questions can help one identify their unique qualities, needs, and preferences, and use this self-knowledge to make informed decisions about their romantic interests and relationship dynamics.

Additionally, it is essential to recognize the role of external factors, such as family, culture, and media, in shaping one's self-concept. For example, growing up in a culture that values physical beauty and social status may influence one's body image and self-esteem. Similarly, exposure to media portrayals of idealized love and relationships may create unrealistic expectations and standards. By acknowledging these influences, individuals can critically evaluate their beliefs and values and modify them if necessary to align with their true selves.

Theme 2: Identifying Your Attachment Style

Attachment theory is a psychological framework that explains how individuals form emotional bonds with others. It proposes that individuals develop certain attachment styles based on their early childhood experiences with their primary caregivers. These attachment styles shape their attitudes, behaviors, and expectations in romantic relationships.

There are four main attachment styles - secure, anxious-preoccupied, dismissive-avoidant, and fearful-avoidant. Secure individuals feel comfortable with intimacy and seek closeness with others without fear of rejection or abandonment. Anxious-preoccupied individuals crave intimacy and fear rejection and abandonment, often resulting in clingy or needy behaviors. Dismissive-avoidant individuals value independence and avoid intimacy to prevent vulnerability and emotional pain. Fearful-avoidant individuals have ambivalent feelings about intimacy, often vacillating between seeking and avoiding closeness due to mistrust and fear of emotional hurt.

Identifying one's attachment style is essential in understanding their emotional needs and communication style in romantic relationships. It can also help individuals recognize maladaptive patterns and seek therapy or counseling to develop healthier attachment behaviors.

Theme 3: Communicating Your Needs and Expectations

Effective communication is a critical component of any successful relationship. This includes understanding one's own needs and expectations and expressing them to their partner. Lack of communication or miscommunication can lead to misunderstandings, conflicts, and dissatisfaction in the relationship.

To communicate effectively, it is essential to use "I" statements instead of "you" statements. For example, instead of saying, "You never listen to me," one can say, "I feel unheard when you interrupt me while I am talking." This approach avoids blame and criticism and focuses on expressing one's feelings and needs.

It is also essential to be assertive but not aggressive or passive. Assertiveness means expressing one's thoughts and feelings in a clear, direct, and respectful manner while acknowledging the other person's perspective. It involves setting boundaries, stating needs, and negotiating solutions to problems.

Finally, it is important to listen actively and empathetically to one's partner and show interest and validation in their feelings and needs. This builds trust, intimacy, and mutual respect in the relationship and fosters emotional connection.

Theme 4: Maintaining Self-Care and Boundaries

In any relationship, individuals may sometimes prioritize their partner's needs and neglect their own self-care and boundaries. This can lead to emotional exhaustion, burnout, and resentment in the long run. It is essential to maintain self-care practices, such as exercise, healthy eating, relaxation, and socialization, to maintain physical and mental well-being.

Setting and maintaining boundaries is also crucial in any relationship. This involves identifying what one is comfortable and uncomfortable with and communicating it to their partner. Boundaries can include personal space, time for oneself, financial issues, and emotional needs. It is important to assess one's own values and priorities and be assertive in maintaining one's boundaries.

Theme 5: Navigating Conflict and Difficult Emotions

Every relationship involves conflicts and difficult emotions, and how individuals handle them can impact the quality and longevity of the relationship. It is essential to recognize one's emotional triggers and communicate them to their partner to avoid misinterpretations and escalations of conflicts.

In addition, individuals need to recognize and regulate their emotions effectively. This involves mindfulness, self-soothing, and self-care practices that help individuals manage their emotions and avoid reacting impulsively or aggressively. It is also essential to practice active listening and empathy to understand one's partner's perspective and find constructive solutions to conflicts.

Theme 6: Cultivating Gratitude and Appreciation

Finally, in the context of finding and sustaining love, cultivating gratitude and appreciation can foster positive emotions, enhance relationship satisfaction, and promote resilience in the face of challenges. Research has shown that couples who express gratitude and appreciation towards each other have higher levels of commitment, trust, and satisfaction in their relationships.

Gratitude involves recognizing and acknowledging one's partner's positive qualities, actions, and contributions and expressing thanks for them. This can include verbal affirmations, small gestures, or thoughtful deeds that show appreciation and affection. It also involves recognizing one's own positive qualities and contributions to the relationship and valuing one's partner's recognition and appreciation of them.

Conclusion

In conclusion, finding and sustaining love requires self-awareness, self-knowledge, and effective communication, among other skills. By understanding one's self-concept, attachment style, needs, and expectations, individuals can cultivate healthier and fulfilling relationships. Additionally, by maintaining self-care, boundaries, and gratitude, individuals can navigate challenges and conflicts in a constructive and positive manner. Thus, it is crucial to engage in self-reflection, self-exploration, and self-improvement as an ongoing process in one's personal and relational growth.

2. Knowing what you want in a partner

Introduction

The search for love is a journey that many embark upon, but not everyone knows what they want in a partner. Knowing what you want in a partner is crucial in choosing and sustaining a healthy relationship. A successful relationship is one that is based on shared goals, values, interests, and beliefs, among other factors. In this paper, we will discuss the importance of knowing what you want in a partner in relation to finding and sustaining love.

Knowing What You Want in a Partner

The first step in finding and sustaining love is knowing what you want in a partner. The process of finding a partner can be frustrating and time-consuming, but it is worth it when you find the right person. Knowing what you want in a partner is essential for several reasons. First, it helps you to identify what you are looking for in a relationship. Secondly, it helps you to avoid wasting time with people who do not fit your criteria. Thirdly, it helps you to attract the right partner who shares your goals and interests in life.

Before starting to look for a partner, it is important to know what you want in a partner. Here are some factors to consider:

1. Shared values and beliefs

Shared values and beliefs are critical for a relationship to work. It is important that you and your partner share similar values and beliefs about life, religion, family, politics, and other important aspects of life. Having similar values and beliefs helps you to make important decisions together and build a strong foundation for the relationship.

2. Personality

Personality plays a major role in attracting and sustaining a healthy relationship. It is important to find a partner who has a personality that complements yours. A partner's personality should be compatible with yours, and they should be able to complement your strengths and weaknesses.

3. Communication style

Communication is essential for a healthy relationship. It is important to find a partner who communicates in a way that is compatible with yours. Some people communicate better in writing, while others prefer face-to-face conversations. It is important to find someone who communicates in a way that makes you feel comfortable and understood.

4. Emotional maturity

Emotional maturity is critical for a healthy relationship. It is important to find a partner who is emotionally mature and able to handle conflicts and difficulties in the relationship. Emotional maturity helps partners to develop a deeper connection and understanding of each other.

5. Interests and hobbies

Shared interests and hobbies are important in a relationship. It is important to find a partner who shares your interests and hobbies, which can help to build a strong connection and allow for fun activities together.

Finding Love

Finding love can be challenging, but it is possible when you know what you want in a partner. Here are some tips for finding love:

1. Be clear about what you want in a partner

Before starting your search for a partner, it is important to be clear about what you want in a partner. Write down the qualities that are important to you and use them as a guide when looking for a partner.

2. Stay open-minded

While it is important to know what you want in a partner, it is important to stay open-minded and not limit yourself to a specific type of person. Be open to meeting people who may not fit your exact criteria but have other wonderful qualities that could be a good fit for you.

3. Put yourself out there

To increase your chances of finding love, it is important to put yourself out there. Join social and professional organizations, attend events, and try online dating. The more you put yourself out there, the more likely you are to meet someone who shares your interests and values.

Sustaining Love

After finding love, it is important to sustain it by building a healthy and long-lasting relationship. Here are some tips for sustaining love:

1. Communicate openly and honestly

Communication is essential for sustaining a healthy relationship. It is important to communicate openly and honestly with your partner about your feelings, emotions, and thoughts. A lack of communication can cause misunderstandings and lead to conflicts in the relationship.

2. Develop trust

Trust is the foundation of a healthy relationship. It is important to develop trust by being honest, reliable, and transparent with your partner. Trust allows for open communication and creates a sense of security and safety in the relationship.

3. Show appreciation and affection

Showing appreciation and affection is important in sustaining love. It is important to express gratitude and show affection towards your partner, whether through small gestures or grand gestures. This creates a positive atmosphere in the relationship, helps to strengthen the bond, and promotes a sense of intimacy.

4. Work through conflicts

Conflicts are inevitable in any relationship, but it is important to work through them and find a resolution that works for both partners. This involves active listening, compromise, and a willingness to understand each other's perspectives.

Conclusion

Knowing what you want in a partner is essential in finding and sustaining love. It helps you to identify what you are looking for in a relationship, avoid wasting time with people who do not fit your criteria, and attract the right partner who shares your goals and interests in life. To find love, it is important to be clear about what you want in a partner, stay open-minded, and put yourself out there. To sustain love, it is important to communicate openly and honestly, develop trust, show appreciation and affection, and work through conflicts. With these tips, you can find and sustain a healthy and long-lasting relationship.

3. Identifying potential partners

Introduction:

Finding and sustaining love can be a challenging and daunting task. Many people struggle with it and often wonder where to find love and how to sustain it once they have found it. It is crucial to identify potential partners and build strong relationships with them. This paper examines the various ways in which individuals can find and sustain love by identifying potential partners.

1. Friends and Family:

One of the best ways to identify potential partners is through your friends and family. They know you better than anyone else and can recommend people they think will be a good match for you. They can also offer advice and support throughout the dating process. It is important to be open-minded and take their suggestions seriously. However, it is essential to keep in mind that not all recommendations will work out.

2. Social Media:

Social media has become a popular tool for finding and sustaining love. Platforms such as Facebook, Instagram, and Twitter can connect individuals with potential partners from all over the world. It is essential to practice caution and be careful when interacting with people online. It is also important to verify their identity and avoid sharing personal information until you have built trust and established a relationship.

3. Professional Networking:

Professional networking events can also provide opportunities for meeting potential partners. Attending industry conferences, trade shows, and other professional events can increase your chances of meeting someone with whom you share a mutual interest. It is important to approach these events with an open attitude and be willing to make new connections.

4. Volunteer Work:

Volunteering is another great way to meet potential partners. Helping others allows individuals to connect with like-minded people and build a sense of community. Volunteering can also provide an opportunity for individuals to showcase their skills and attributes while getting to know others who share similar values and goals.

5. Online Dating:

Online dating has revolutionized the way individuals find potential partners. Dating sites and apps such as Tinder, Bumble, and eHarmony have made it easier for people to connect with each other. It is important to be honest and upfront when creating a profile and engaging with potential matches. It is also important to use caution and be aware of scams and fraudulent activity.

6. Hobbies and Interests:

Finally, hobbies and interests can also provide opportunities for meeting potential partners. Joining a club or group that aligns with your interests can connect you to like-minded individuals who share your passions. It is important to approach these activities with an open attitude and be willing to try new things.

Sustaining Love:

Once individuals have identified potential partners, it is essential to sustain the relationship. Here are some ways to build and maintain a healthy and long-lasting relationship:

1. Communication:

Communication is the foundation of any healthy relationship. It is essential to communicate effectively and openly with your partner. Be honest about your feelings, needs, and expectations, and listen actively when your partner speaks. Remember to express appreciation and gratitude frequently.

2. Trust:

Trust is another critical component of a healthy relationship. It is important to be trustworthy and also to trust your partner. Establish boundaries and respect each other's privacy. Avoid jealousy or possessiveness, and be willing to give your partner the benefit of the doubt.

3. Quality Time:

Spending quality time together is essential for maintaining a healthy relationship. It is important to create opportunities for meaningful and enjoyable experiences. Whether it's going on a date, taking a walk, or watching a movie, make time for activities that you both enjoy.

4. Respect:

Respect is crucial in any relationship. It is important to treat your partner with kindness, empathy, and understanding. Avoid judgment or criticism, and be willing to see things from their perspective. Keep in mind that everyone has different opinions and beliefs, and that's okay.

5. Intimacy:

Physical intimacy is an important aspect of any romantic relationship. It is important to be open-minded, respectful, and communicative about your physical needs and desires. Develop a level of comfort and trust when exploring physical intimacy.

6. Compromise:

Compromise is another essential ingredient for a healthy relationship. Be willing to find common ground and work through conflicts together. Avoid being rigid or inflexible, and be willing to negotiate and find solutions that work for both partners.

Conclusion:

Identifying potential partners is an important step in finding and sustaining love. There are many strategies for meeting potential partners, including friends and family, social media, professional networking, volunteer work, online dating, and hobbies and interests. Once individuals have identified potential partners, it is important to build and maintain a healthy and long-lasting relationship through effective communication, trust, quality time, respect, physical intimacy, and compromise. By following these strategies, individuals can increase their chances of finding and sustaining a meaningful and fulfilling romantic relationship.

4. Effective communication and flirting

Introduction

Effective communication and flirting are two key factors in finding and sustaining love. As humans, we have a need to connect with others, especially those we are romantically interested in. However, many people struggle with effective communication and flirting skills, hindering their ability to find and keep a relationship. In this paper, we will discuss the importance of effective communication and flirting in finding and sustaining love, as well as strategies for improving in these areas.

Effective Communication

Effective communication is critical in any relationship, especially romantic relationships. Communication is how we express our thoughts, feelings, and needs to others. Therefore, it is important that we communicate our emotions and needs clearly and effectively. Effective communication ensures that our partner understands us, which can prevent misunderstandings and conflicts.

One of the most important aspects of effective communication in romantic relationships is listening. Listening ensures that our partner feels heard and valued, which strengthens the bond between partners. It also helps us understand our partner's perspective, which can prevent conflicts from arising. However, listening is not merely waiting for our turn to speak. It requires active engagement, which means that we pay attention to what our partner is saying and respond appropriately.

Another aspect of effective communication is speaking honestly. Honesty is key in building trust with our partner. By communicating honestly, we can convey our emotions and needs in a way that is genuine and authentic. This can also help prevent misunderstandings and conflicts.

Flirting

Flirting is the process of showing romantic interest in another person. It is a playful way of showing someone that you are interested in them. Flirting can help build attraction and chemistry between partners. However, it is important to flirt in a respectful and appropriate way.

One way to effectively flirt is to use humor. Humor is a great way to break the ice and make our partner feel at ease. It can also showcase our personality, making us more attractive to our partner. However, it is important to use humor in a respectful way, as inappropriate jokes or comments can be offensive.

Another way to flirt is to use body language. Body language can convey our interest and attraction in subtle ways. For example, maintaining eye contact, leaning in, and touching our partner's arm or hand can all communicate interest. However, it is important to use body language in a respectful way, as inappropriate touching or invading personal space can be uncomfortable or offensive.

Flirting is a delicate balance. It can help build attraction and chemistry between partners, but it can also backfire if done inappropriately. Therefore, it is important to be respectful and appropriate when flirting.

Finding Love

Effective communication and flirting are important tools in finding love. Effective communication ensures that we are able to express our emotions and needs in a way that is clear and authentic, making us more attractive to potential partners. Listening and honesty are two key aspects of effective communication that can help us build trust and understanding with our partner.

Flirting is also important in finding love. It can help build attraction and chemistry between partners, making us more likely to connect romantically with someone. However, it is important to use flirting in a respectful and appropriate way, as inappropriate behavior can be offensive.

Sustaining Love

Effective communication and flirting are not only important in finding love, but they are also critical in sustaining love. In order to sustain a relationship, effective communication is essential. It ensures that both partners can express their emotions and needs, which can prevent conflicts and misunderstandings.

Honesty is especially important in sustaining a relationship. It allows both partners to trust each other, which can help strengthen the bond between them. However, it is important to be honest in a respectful way, as brutal honesty can be hurtful.

Flirting is also important in sustaining a relationship. It can help keep the romance alive and prevent partners from becoming complacent in their relationship. However, it is important to adapt flirting to the stage of the relationship. For example, flirting may be more reserved in a committed, long-term relationship than in the early stages of dating.

Improving Communication and Flirting Skills

Improving communication and flirting skills can be a challenge for many people. However, there are strategies that can be used to improve in these areas.

One way to improve communication skills is to practice active listening. This means paying full attention to what our partner is saying and responding appropriately. It can also be helpful to repeat what our partner has said to ensure that we have understood them correctly.

Another way to improve communication skills is to be mindful of our tone and body language. Nonverbal communication can be just as important as verbal communication. For example, crossing our arms or rolling our eyes can convey defensiveness or frustration, which can prevent effective communication.

To improve flirting skills, it can be helpful to practice in a safe environment, such as with friends or in a social setting. This can help build confidence and allow us to experiment with different types of flirting.

Another way to improve flirting skills is to pay attention to our partner's body language. This can help us gauge their interest and respond appropriately. For example, if our partner seems uncomfortable with physical touch, it may be best to dial back the flirting until they are more comfortable.

Conclusion

Effective communication and flirting are critical in finding and sustaining love. Effective communication ensures that both partners can express their emotions and needs in a way that is clear and authentic. Listening and honesty are two key aspects of effective communication that can help build trust and understanding with our partner. Flirting can help build attraction and chemistry between partners, but it is important to be respectful and appropriate. Improving communication and flirting skills can be challenging, but practicing active listening, being mindful of tone and body language, and paying attention to our partner's body language can all help improve in these areas.

5. Dating strategies

Dating strategies in relation to how to find and sustain love

Introduction:

Dating is a common term used to describe the process of meeting someone new with the intention of exploring a potential romantic relationship. For those who are single, dating can be an exciting opportunity to get to know yourself better and meet new people. However, for many individuals, the process of dating can be stressful and overwhelming. With so many potential partners available, finding and sustaining love can be a difficult task. In this paper, we will discuss dating strategies in relation to how to find and sustain love. We will examine common obstacles to finding and sustaining love, as well as tips for success in the dating world.

Obstacles to Finding and Sustaining Love:

Before discussing dating strategies for success, it is important to understand some common obstacles that can hinder individuals' ability to find and sustain love. Some of these obstacles include:

1. Fear of vulnerability: Many individuals fear being vulnerable in a relationship. This fear often stems from past experiences, such as

heartbreak or rejection. However, if we are not willing to be vulnerable, we cannot fully connect with another person.

2. Unrealistic expectations: Unrealistic expectations can lead to disappointment and frustration. It is important to understand that no one is perfect, and all relationships require work.

3. Lack of self-awareness: Understanding our own needs, wants, and values is crucial in building a healthy and lasting relationship. Without self-awareness, it is easy to fall into unhealthy patterns of behavior and find ourselves in unfulfilling relationships.

4. Poor communication skills: Communication is the cornerstone of any healthy relationship. Without effective communication, misunderstandings and conflicts can arise, causing unnecessary stress and strain on the relationship.

Tips for Finding Love:

Now that we have discussed some common obstacles to finding and sustaining love, let's explore some tips for success in the dating world. Some of these include:

1. Be open-minded: It is important to be open-minded when it comes to dating. This means being open to different types of people and

experiences. You never know who you might meet and how they may impact your life.

2. Practice self-love: Before we can fully love someone else, we must first love ourselves. This means taking care of our physical, emotional, and mental health. When we love ourselves, we attract others who share our positive energy.

3. Take things slow: It is important to take things slow when it comes to dating. Rushing into a relationship can lead to unrealistic expectations and disappointment. Take the time to get to know someone and build a strong foundation before committing to a relationship.

4. Communicate effectively: Communication is key in any healthy relationship. Be honest about your needs, wants, and values, and listen to your partner's as well. Avoid making assumptions and clarify misunderstandings as they arise.

5. Have fun: Dating should be fun and enjoyable. Don't take it too seriously and allow yourself to have a good time. View dating as an opportunity to learn more about yourself and what you want in a partner.

Tips for Sustaining Love:

Once you have found a partner and established a strong relationship, it is important to sustain love over time. Some tips for doing so include:

1. Continue to communicate effectively: Effective communication is just as important in a long-term relationship as it is in the beginning stages. Continue to be honest with your partner about your wants and needs, and work together to solve problems as they arise.

2. Show appreciation: It is important to regularly show appreciation for your partner. This can be in the form of verbal affirmations, acts of service, or small gifts. Expressing gratitude and appreciation goes a long way in sustaining a healthy and happy relationship.

3. Spend quality time together: Spending quality time together is essential in any relationship. This can be in the form of date nights, weekend getaways, or even just a quiet night at home. Make time for each other, and prioritize each other's needs and wants.

4. Keep things interesting: Over time, relationships can become routine and predictable. It is important to keep things interesting and maintain a sense of adventure. This can be in the form of trying new activities or hobbies together, spicing up your sex life, or simply trying a new restaurant or travel destination.

Conclusion:

In conclusion, finding and sustaining love can be a difficult task. However, with the right mindset and strategies, it is possible to build a healthy and lasting relationship. By understanding common obstacles to finding and sustaining love, and implementing tips for success, individuals can increase their chances of finding and sustaining a fulfilling relationship. Remember to be open-minded, practice self-love, communicate effectively, and prioritize each other's needs and wants. With these strategies in mind, anyone can find and sustain love.

6. A list of places to seek love

Love is a powerful emotion and one that people across the globe seek to experience. However, it is not always easy to find and sustain love. For some, it seems like they find love without even trying, while for others, it remains an elusive dream. There are certain places and activities that can help increase the chances of finding and sustaining love. In this article, we will explore a list of six such places and how they can be advantageous in your quest to find love.

1. Online dating platforms

The emergence of online dating platforms has revolutionized the dating scene. These platforms have made it easier for people to find love by allowing them to connect with a wider pool of potential partners. Online dating platforms such as Match.com, OkCupid, and eHarmony offer extensive questionnaires that help you get to know your potential partner's likes, interests, hobbies, and values. This in-depth understanding makes it easier to find compatible matches.

Furthermore, online dating platforms offer a level of anonymity that allows people to feel more comfortable and confident when pursuing romantic relationships. It is important to exercise caution when using these platforms and ensure that you take the time to get to know your potential partner before meeting them in person.

2. Social gatherings

Social gatherings such as parties, weddings, and networking events offer a great opportunity to meet potential partners. The relaxed and informal atmosphere of these events makes it easier to interact with others and get to know them better. Being social and engaging with people at these events can help you build meaningful connections with those who share similar interests and values.

Moreover, attending events that align with your interests can increase the likelihood of meeting someone with similar interests and values. For instance, if you love music, attending concerts or music festivals could connect you to someone with a similar passion.

3. Volunteering and charity events

Volunteering for charitable causes not only contributes to a good cause but also provides an opportunity to meet like-minded individuals who share similar values and interests. Volunteering and charity events are filled with people who genuinely care about making the world a better place and are interested in connecting with others who share the same values.

Volunteering also provides an opportunity to network with people from different walks of life and can help expand your social circle. Additionally, volunteering can help build self-confidence and a sense of purpose, making you a more desirable partner.

4. Fitness and wellness activities

Fitness and wellness activities such as yoga, meditation classes, or gym workouts can provide an excellent opportunity to find love. These activities not only promote physical well-being but also encourage mental and emotional balance. Participating in such activities increases your chances of meeting someone who values health and wellness and shares similar interests.

Additionally, engaging in fitness and wellness activities can boost your self-esteem, improve your appearance, and make you more confident and attractive to potential partners. It is a great way to improve both your physical and mental health while also increasing your chances of finding love.

5. Educational and cultural events

Educational and cultural events such as lectures, workshops, and art exhibitions can bring together people with a shared interest in a particular topic. These events stimulate intellectual and cultural curiosity and offer an opportunity to meet people who share similar interests and values.

Attending these events can help you expand your knowledge and challenge your perspectives. It is a great way to engage with people who are passionate about learning and discovering new things. Furthermore, intellectual conversations with like-minded individuals can spark romantic connections.

6. Traveling

Traveling is a fantastic way to broaden your horizons and engage with people from different cultures and backgrounds. It provides a unique opportunity to step outside your comfort zone, experience new things, and make new connections.

Traveling solo is an excellent way to meet people from different walks of life and offers a chance to connect with locals and other travelers. It is an adventure that can not only help you find love but also challenge and inspire you to grow and develop as a person.

Conclusion

Finding and sustaining love is a journey that requires patience, effort, and an open mind. The places mentioned in this list offer unique opportunities to connect with like-minded individuals and increase your chances of finding lasting love. However, it is important to remember that love cannot be forced, and it is essential to focus on personal growth and self-love regardless of your relationship status. With an open heart and mind, you can create a beautiful and fulfilling romantic connection that lasts a lifetime.

7. Quiz

1. What is the first step in finding love?

A. Creating a dating profile
   B. Developing self-love and confidence
   C. Asking friends to set you up
   D. Going out to bars and clubs

2. Which of the following is important in attracting a partner?

A. Having a lot of money
   B. Being physically perfect
   C. Being true to yourself
   D. Pretending to be someone you're not

3. How can you increase your chances of finding love?

A. Lowering your standards
   B. Staying indoors all the time
   C. Meeting new people
   D. Being stingy with your emotions

4. How should you approach first dates?

A. Being overly critical of your date
   B. Being too eager to please
   C. Being honest and open
   D. Being aggressive and pushy

5. How can you tell if someone is a good match for you?

A. They have a lot of money
   B. They are exactly like you
   C. They share similar interests and values
   D. They are extremely attractive

Answers: 1B, 2C, 3C, 4C, 5C.

III. Building a Relationship

1. Establishing trust and respect

Introduction

Love is a complex concept that continues to perplex humanity. It could be argued that love is the most common and most sought-after aspect of the human experience. Everyone wants to find true love and sustain it. Love builds trust and respect, which are two essential elements that sustain relationships. Trust and respect are vital ingredients that keep a relationship strong, making it important to know how to establish trust and respect in relationships. This essay discusses the importance of trust and respect in relationships and provides strategies on how to find and sustain love through establishing these two key elements.

The Importance of Trust and Respect in Relationships

Trust and respect are the foundation of any successful relationship. When partners establish trust and respect in their relationship, they build a bond that enables them to connect with each other at a deeper level. Trust and respect are the glue that holds a relationship together. Without these two elements, a relationship is likely to end in disaster. Many people end their relationships because they lack trust and respect for their partner.

Trust is built on honesty, integrity, and consistency. When partners are honest with each other, they build trust. They are transparent about their motives, actions, and intentions. Being consistent with one's actions and words also builds trust. If a partner says they will do something, they should do it. Trust can be easily eroded when promises are not kept, or when one partner is not honest with the other.

Respect is another fundamental element that sustains relationships. When partners respect each other, they value each other's beliefs, thoughts, and opinions. Respect fosters a sense of love and appreciation, which creates a positive atmosphere in the relationship. Respect allows partners to communicate effectively and constructively, which strengthens their bond. When partners respect each other, they are willing to listen to each other's point of view and work together to find solutions to problems.

Establishing Trust and Respect in Relationships

Establishing trust and respect in relationships requires effort and commitment. It involves creating an environment that is conducive to building and maintaining trust and respect. Here are some strategies on how to establish trust and respect in relationships:

1. Be Honest: Honesty is the foundation of trust. Be honest with your partner about your feelings, your thoughts, and your actions. Share your feelings and thoughts openly. Be clear and concise in your communication. When your partner knows that you are honest with them, they feel more comfortable and secure, which builds trust.

2. Be Reliable: Reliability builds trust. If you promise to do something, do it. If you commit to a plan, stick to it. Be consistent in your actions and words. When your partner knows that they can rely on you, they feel more secure and confident, which builds trust.

3. Show Empathy: Empathy is essential in building respect. Try to understand your partner's perspective, thoughts, and feelings. Put yourself in their shoes and try to see things from their point of view. Show your partner that you are listening by reacting to what they say. When you show empathy, you show that you respect and value your partner's thoughts and feelings.

4. Be Open-Minded: Being open-minded is crucial in building respect. Be willing to consider your partner's opinions and ideas. Be open to new experiences, thoughts, and beliefs. When you are open-minded, you show that you respect and value your partner's beliefs and opinions.

5. Communicate Effectively: Effective communication is essential in building trust and respect. Be clear and concise in your communication. Avoid making assumptions or jumping to conclusions. Be willing to listen actively and give your partner your full attention. When you communicate effectively, you establish a foundation of trust and respect.

Strategies to Find and Sustain Love

Finding and sustaining love requires effort and commitment. It involves building trust and respect and maintaining them over time. Here are some strategies to find and sustain love:

1. Identify Your Needs and Wants: Before you can find love, you need to identify your needs and wants. What qualities do you want in a partner? What are your deal breakers? Knowing your needs and wants will help you find someone who is compatible with you and who shares your values and beliefs.

2. Be Authentic: Be yourself. Do not pretend to be someone you are not to impress someone. You want to find someone who likes you for who you are, not for who you pretend to be. When you are authentic, you build trust by being honest and transparent.

3. Take Your Time: Finding love takes time. Do not rush into a relationship. Take time to get to know someone before committing to a relationship. It takes time to build trust and respect, so be patient and allow the relationship to develop naturally.

4. Communicate Effectively: Effective communication is essential in sustaining love. Be clear and concise in your communication. Be open to listening to your partner's perspective. Be willing to compromise and find solutions to problems together.

5. Show Appreciation: Showing appreciation is essential in sustaining love. Show your partner that you value and respect them. Be grateful for the little things they do and express your gratitude often. When you show appreciation, you reinforce the bond of trust and respect that sustains the relationship.

Conclusion

In conclusion, establishing trust and respect is essential in finding and sustaining love. Trust and respect are the foundation of any successful relationship. If you want to find and sustain love, you need to build trust and respect with your partner. It takes effort and commitment to establish and maintain trust and respect, but the rewards are worth it. When you have trust and respect in your relationship, you create a strong bond that can withstand any challenge. By following the strategies discussed in this essay, you can establish and sustain a loving relationship built on trust and respect.

2. Improving communication skills

Introduction

Before delving into the topic, it is important to understand that communication is a fundamental aspect of any successful relationship. Good communication promotes understanding, trust, and intimacy. It allows partners to provide emotional support, work through conflicts, and share their thoughts and feelings. In contrast, poor communication can lead to misunderstandings, conflicts, and ultimately, the breakdown of a relationship. This paper aims to explore the importance of communication in finding and sustaining love, while providing practical tips on how to improve communication skills.

Effective Communication in Finding Love

When it comes to finding love, communication is key. Whether you are searching for a romantic partner through online dating, social events, or mutual connections, good communication skills are essential. Here are some tips on how to improve communication when looking for love:

1. Be Clear and Honest

It is important to be clear and honest about who you are and what you are looking for in a relationship. Avoid pretending to be someone you are not just to impress your potential partner. This can result in misunderstandings and eventual disappointment. Clearly communicate your values, beliefs, and expectations from the outset.

2. Listen Carefully

Listening is an essential skill when it comes to communication. Active listening shows that you are interested in what your potential partner has to say, and it allows you to understand their perspectives better. Try to avoid interrupting, and take the time to reflect on what your partner is saying before responding.

3. Ask Questions

Asking questions is an excellent way to show interest and keep the conversation going. It can also help you to gain a better understanding of your partner's thoughts and feelings. However, it is important to remember to ask open-ended questions to encourage a more detailed response.

4. Be Respectful

Respect is key when it comes to communication, especially in the early stages of a relationship. Be mindful of your tone, facial expressions, and body language to ensure that you are not conveying disrespect or belittling your partner's thoughts and feelings.

5. Be Present

Be fully present in the moment when communicating with your partner. Avoid distractions such as checking your phone or engaging in non-verbal cues that show a lack of interest. This will show your partner that you value their time and opinion.

Effective Communication in Sustaining Love

Communication is an ongoing process in any relationship, and in order to sustain a healthy and fulfilling love life, it is important to maintain good communication skills. Here are some tips on how to improve communication in existing relationships:

1. Allocate Quality Time

Allocate quality time to spend with your partner, where you can connect and share your thoughts and feelings. This could be a date night, a walk, or even simple household chores such as cooking together.

2. Be Open and Honest

Honesty is the best policy when it comes to communication. Try to be open and honest with your partner, even if it may cause conflict. This will help to build trust and intimacy in the relationship.

3. Be a Good Listener

Active listening is just as important in sustaining a relationship as it is in finding one. This means taking the time to truly understand your partner's perspective and allowing them to express their thoughts and feelings.

4. Encourage Feedback

Encourage your partner to provide feedback on your communication style. This will allow you to understand any areas you may need to improve on, and how you can better support your partner.

5. Learn to Compromise

Compromise is important in any relationship and is essential for effective communication. Try to understand your partner's perspective and work together to find a solution that works for both of you.

6. Manage Conflict

Conflict is inevitable in any relationship, but it is important to manage it effectively. This means avoiding blame, being respectful when communicating, and taking time to calm down before discussing the issue.

Conclusion

In conclusion, communication is an essential aspect of finding and sustaining love. By improving communication skills, individuals can enhance their ability to connect with others on a deeper level, thus leading to more fulfilling and healthier relationships. Effective communication involves active listening, asking questions, being respectful, being honest, and allocating quality time. Hence, feel free to implement these practical tips and improve your communication skills to find and sustain love.

3. Navigating conflicts and disagreements

Navigating Conflicts and Disagreements in Relation to How to Find and Sustain Love

Introduction

Navigating conflicts and disagreements in relationships is one of the critical success factors in finding and sustaining love. Love is a complex phenomenon that requires attention, care, and understanding. A relationship can experience challenges and conflicts, and how such situations are handled can impact the longevity and stability of the relationship. This paper discusses how to navigate conflicts and disagreements in the context of finding and sustaining love.

The Importance of Navigating Conflicts and Disagreements in Relationships

Conflicts and disagreements are inevitable in any relationship. Love does not shield individuals from arguments, differences, and misunderstandings. In fact, disagreements are necessary as they present opportunities for growth, learning, and understanding. Additionally, disagreements are signs that individuals may have different values, perspectives, and expectations regarding love and relationships.

Navigating conflicts and disagreements is crucial in finding and sustaining love for various reasons. First, it promotes effective communication and establishes boundaries. Disagreements present opportunities to communicate effectively by sharing information, perspectives, and experiences. This open communication promotes understanding and establishes boundaries that guide the relationship. Secondly, navigating conflicts and disagreements fosters healthy problem solving. Through disagreements, individuals can identify challenges that require solutions, and effective problem-solving can strengthen the relationship. Thirdly, navigating conflicts and disagreements encourages empathy, respect, and trust. Empathy involves understanding the other person's feelings and perspectives, respect involves honoring their opinions and boundaries, while trust involves believing in their intentions and actions.

Strategies for Navigating Conflicts and Disagreements in Relationships

1. Active Listening

Active listening is a critical component of navigating conflicts and disagreements. Active listening involves understanding the other person's perspective and being present for the conversation. It is essential to actively listen to not only the words spoken but also the tone and nonverbal cues. Listening actively promotes understanding and empathy, leading to effective problem-solving.

2. Avoid Blaming or Judging

When individuals get into disagreements, it is common to play the blame game. Blaming and judging, however, do not promote resolution or understanding. Instead, these behaviors can create resentment and further complicate the conflict. It is crucial to avoid blame and judgment and focus on listening and understanding.

3. Avoid Interrupting

Interrupting is another common behavior during disagreements. It can be a sign of disrespect, and it hinders effective communication. Interrupting can prevent individuals from expressing their perspectives and may lead to misunderstandings. It is vital to avoid interrupting and give the other person space to communicate their thoughts.

4. Focus on Understanding Rather than Winning

Disagreements should not be about winning or being right. It is crucial to focus on understanding the other person's perspective and finding solutions that work for both individuals. When the focus is on winning, it can lead to a power struggle that may damage the relationship.

5. Take Responsibility for One's Actions

Taking responsibility for one's actions is essential in navigating conflicts and disagreements. Individuals must own up to their mistakes and apologize when necessary. Taking responsibility demonstrates maturity, and it promotes trust, respect, and honesty.

6. Set Boundaries

Navigating conflicts and disagreements requires setting boundaries. Boundaries are guidelines for the relationship that can help prevent misunderstandings and promote harmony. For example, individuals can set boundaries regarding communication, personal space, and expectations.

7. Use "I" Statements

"I" statements can be helpful in navigating conflicts and disagreements. "I" statements focus on the individual's feelings and perceptions rather than blaming the other person. For example, instead of saying, "You hurt me when you said that," one can say, "I felt hurt when I heard that." "I" statements promote effective communication, prevent misunderstandings, and encourage empathy.

8. Take a Break

Sometimes, navigating conflicts and disagreements can be overwhelming and emotionally draining. It is crucial to know when to take a break and regroup. Taking a break can help individuals calm down, reflect, and come back to the conversation with a clear mind and open heart.

Conclusion

Navigating conflicts and disagreements is crucial in finding and sustaining love. Conflicts and disagreements provide opportunities for growth, understanding, and problem-solving. Effective communication, empathy, respect, and trust are essential in navigating conflicts and disagreements. The strategies discussed in this paper, such as active listening, avoiding blame and judgment, setting boundaries, using "I" statements, and taking a break, can be helpful in navigating conflicts and disagreements. With these strategies, individuals can build strong, healthy, and lasting relationships based on mutual understanding, respect, and love.

4. Balancing independence and interdependence

Introduction

Balancing independence and interdependence is one of the most challenging parts of building successful relationships. Independence means that individuals are self-reliant and able to live and act without relying on others, while interdependence refers to mutual reliance and support in relationships. The challenge is to strike a balance between the two, so that partners can find love and happiness.

This paper looks at the concept of balancing independence and interdependence in relation to finding and sustaining love. It provides an in-depth analysis of how individuals can build healthy relationships while balancing their needs for independence and interdependence.

Understanding Independence and Interdependence

Individuals who are independent tend to be self-sufficient and prefer to make decisions for themselves. They take responsibility for their life and actions and are comfortable with their own company. They do not rely on others for validation and are not easily swayed by other people's opinions. Independence is highly valued in many cultures, and people who are independent are often viewed as strong and resilient.

In contrast, interdependence refers to the need for connection and support from others. People who are interdependent place a high value on relationships and are often highly attuned to other people's needs. They seek out social interactions and place a high value on community and teamwork. Interdependence is often seen as a positive trait in relationships as it promotes empathy, understanding, and cooperation.

Finding and Sustaining Love through independence and Interdependence

Finding love requires individuals to strike a balance between their independence and interdependence needs. Here are some ways individuals can find and sustain love through a balance of independence and interdependence.

1. Build a Strong Sense of Self

The foundation of any successful relationship is a strong sense of self. Individuals who have a strong sense of self are more likely to be independent and assertive, which makes them more attractive and self-assured. Building a sense of self requires individuals to spend time alone and introspect. When people are comfortable in their own company, they are less likely to settle for unhealthy relationships just to avoid being alone.

2. Communicate Effectively

Effective communication is critical in building healthy relationships. Being able to express oneself freely and assertively and listening actively are essential skills in building strong bonds. When individuals are clear about their needs and boundaries, they create healthy interdependence patterns, allowing the relationship to flourish.

3. Support Each Other's Growth

Supporting each other's growth as individuals strengthens the bonds between partners. When partners support each other's growth, they create a balance between interdependence and independence. The partner's growth should be a priority for both in finding and sustaining true love, while finding the necessary balance between independence and interdependence.

4. Set Mutual Goals

Setting mutual goals encourages individuals to work together to achieve them. When people work together towards shared goals, they create healthy interdependence patterns, strengthening the relationship. Working towards a common goal helps each partner to understand each other's strengths and weaknesses, and building trust to help each other improve.

5. Recognize and Celebrate Each Other's Achievements.

Celebrating each other's achievements strengthens feelings of interdependence. Partners who celebrate each other's milestones and accomplishments reinforce their bonds. Acknowledging and celebrating each other's personal growth is an essential part of sustaining love and creating healthy co-dependency in relationships.

6. Spend Time Apart

Spending time apart is essential for maintaining independence in relationships. Independent partners need space to pursue their interests and hobbies without feeling guilty. Spending time apart allows each person to maintain their sense of identity while strengthening their interdependence bond.

Conclusion

Balancing independence and interdependence is vital to finding and sustaining love. It requires individuals to strike a balance between their need for autonomy and their desire for connection. Finding the right balance between independence and interdependence requires self-awareness, good communication skills, mutual support, goals alignment, and acknowledging each other's achievements. It is possible to maintain independence in a relationship and still strengthen the bonds of interdependence. When people find this balance, they create successful and long-lasting relationships filled with love and mutual respect.

5. Intimacy and affection

Intimacy and affection are two essential components that play a crucial role in the development and sustenance of lasting relationships. They are critical for the formation of emotional connections that strengthen bonds and foster deeper levels of trust and understanding between partners. Intimacy refers to the state of being emotionally close to someone, while cuddling, holding hands, kissing, and hugging are examples of affection. In this essay, we will explore the significance of intimacy and affection in finding and sustaining love.

The Importance of Intimacy in Relationships

Intimacy is a quality that is essential for the formation of strong emotional ties. However, it is not an easy task to achieve and maintain. One must be vulnerable and open with their partner while also being willing to listen and communicate effectively. It is through this openness that couples can create a shared sense of trust that can ultimately bring them even closer together.

Intimacy involves developing a deep sense of empathy towards one's partner. It requires being present and allowing yourself to be vulnerable to your partner while also being empathetic and attentive. Intimacy can help boost self-esteem and promote a positive sense of self-awareness, leading to a greater sense of self-esteem, happiness, and fulfilment.

Intimacy is not merely a physical act alone; it includes sharing one's thoughts and feelings. Sharing personal stories and discussing one's innermost thoughts and feelings with one's partner can strengthen the emotional connection between them, leading to a deeper level of intimacy. Once that trust is formed, it paves the way for the arousal of sexual attraction between partners.

The Importance of Affection in Relationships

Affection is a crucial tenet of any intimate relationship. It provides partners with a sense of warmth and comfort and creates a deep sense of closeness. A loving touch, a warm hug, or a passionate kiss can speak volumes of one's feelings towards their significant other.

Affection can be expressed in many ways. One can hold hands while walking, wrap their arms around their partner while sitting or standing, or give a warm embrace when parting ways. These actions help perpetuate feelings of love and affection and can help promote a deeper connection between partners.

Affection can also serve as an affirmation of one's love for their partner. Simple gestures such as leaving a love note, being attentive and observant to their needs, or preparing a special meal can go a long way in communicating your love for your partner. An expression of affection reassures one's partner of their worth and value in the relationship and strengthens the emotional bond between them.

Sustaining Love Through Intimacy and Affection

Intimacy and affection are essential aspects of any relationship, regardless of its duration or nature. It is not uncommon for people to experience a decline in the level of intimacy and affection in a relationship over time, which may have negative effects on the relationship's overall health and longevity.

Sustaining love requires actively working towards maintaining and increasing the intimacy and affection in the relationship. One of the most important steps is communication. Discussing one's needs and expectations concerning intimacy and affection can help both partners develop a better understanding of each other's needs and desires.

Partners should also be willing to be receptive to their partner's demands and needs. They should be open to trying new things, including physical intimacy, to keep the relationship fresh and exciting. Engaging in shared activities such as hiking, traveling, or attending cultural events can also help promote intimacy and affection in relationships.

Couples should also make a conscious effort to show affection towards one another regularly. Simple gestures such as holding hands, hugging, and kissing can go a long way in reinforcing the love and emotional connection between partners. Remembering special dates such as anniversaries or birthdays and going out of your way to make these days special can also promote affection in the relationship.

Other factors that may help promote intimacy and affection in relationships include positive communication, making time for each other, creating shared goals, and showing appreciation for one another. Couples that focus on building these habits tend to have relationships that are more meaningful, satisfying, and long-lasting.

Conclusion

In conclusion, intimacy and affection are two vital components of any healthy relationship, and they play essential roles in finding and sustaining love. Intimacy helps create deep emotional connections between partners, while affection cements the emotional bond and provides reassurance of one's love for their partner. Sustaining love requires active communication, openness, and a willingness to be vulnerable with one's partner. It also involves making time for each other, engaging in shared activities, and showing appreciation for each other regularly. Couples that engage in these habits tend to have relationships that are more fulfilling, meaningful, and long-lasting. When intimacy and affection are present in a relationship, profound emotional ties can be established between partners, which creates a foundation of love and trust that can last a lifetime.

6. Power games in relationships

Introduction

Love is undoubtedly an essential component of our lives, and everyone desires it. However, finding love and sustaining it can be challenging, and power games in relationships can make it even more complicated. Power games refer to the tactics people use to gain control and dominance over their partners or significant others. Such power struggles are often detrimental to relationships, leading to misunderstandings, arguments, and sometimes breakups. Therefore, understanding power games and how to avoid them is crucial for individuals seeking to find and sustain love. In this paper, we will explore how power games affect relationships and examine ways to build and maintain healthy relationships.

Power Games in Relationships

Power games can take many forms, and they are often subtle but can be destructive. One common power game in relationships is the use of manipulation to control one's partner. This can take various forms, such as emotional blackmail, guilt trips, threat-making, or withholding love or affection. Manipulation can be carried out by both men and women, and it often begins subtly, with minor demands that grow over time.

Another power game common in relationships is the silent treatment. This involves emotional withdrawal, where one person stops communication with their partner. The silent treatment aims to make the other person feel guilty, anxious, or insecure and is usually a form of emotional manipulation.

Financial power games are also common in relationships, with one partner using their financial resources to control or dominate the other. This can take various forms, such as withholding funds, restricting access to finances, or insisting on their partner being financially dependent on them. Such behavior can lead to resentment and tension in relationships.

In addition, physical dominance is another form of power game in relationships. This can involve intimidation through physical violence or threats, such as pounding fists or screaming.

How Power Games Affect Relationships

Power games have a profound impact on relationships, often leading to negative outcomes. These negative outcomes include arguments, emotional instability, and ultimately breaking up.

Power games often lead to mistrust in relationships. The person who feels controlled may begin to question their partner's motives and lose faith in the relationship. Similarly, the person who is looking to exert control may begin to suspect that their partner is not fully committed to the relationship, leading to insecurity and distrust.

Power games can also cause emotional damage to individuals. Manipulation, emotional blackmail, and the silent treatment, for example, can be emotionally taxing. They lead to feelings of isolation, anxiety, and depression, and can eventually end up harming the mental health of individuals.

Furthermore, financial power games and physical dominance can create a sense of inequality in relationships. This can lead to feelings of worthlessness and low self-esteem, especially if the affected person puts up with these behaviors due to a lack of resources or independence.

The impact of power games can be significant and long-lasting, and unfortunately, it can be challenging to recover from them fully.

How to Build and Maintain a Healthy Relationship

A healthy relationship requires effort and commitment from both parties involved. To create a healthy relationship, it is essential to identify power games and avoid them proactively. Here are some ways to build and maintain a healthy relationship.

1. Communication

Communication is critical in any relationship. It is essential to establish open and honest communication to avoid any misunderstandings, mistrust, or power struggles. Communicating your expectations, feelings, and needs can help build mutual respect and trust. It's important to listen and respond appropriately to your partner's concerns, challenges, and ideas.

2. Mutual Respect

Mutual respect is crucial in any relationship. Both partners should respect each other's feelings, choices, and decisions. When either of the partners makes decisions, it should be done with consideration of the other person's views. Mutual respect creates an environment of trust and ensures both parties are on an equal footing.

3. Trust

Trust is the foundation of all relationships. Trust is built over time and requires consistent effort from both parties to establish and maintain. One person cannot trust the other without a reason, and it's important to take actions and display behavior that fosters trust. Trust is important to establish a healthy relationship and helps to create a sense of security.

4. Avoiding power games

Power games can be detrimental to a relationship and should be avoided. It's essential to take a proactive approach to identify and avoid such games, whether emotional, financial, or physical. Couples should seek to establish mutual understanding and respect and find ways to avoid such behaviors that can cause power struggles.

5. Supporting Each other

Supporting each other in times of need is another critical aspect of building a healthy relationship. It is essential to be empathetic and understanding, even in challenging situations. Being there for your partner and providing support strengthens a relationship, and promotes a sense of teamwork.

Conclusion

In conclusion, power games pose a significant threat to relationships, leading to feelings of mistrust, emotional damage, and an overall breakdown of the relationship. Healthy relationships require effort from both parties to establish respect, trust, communication, support, and a sense of equality. By proactively avoiding power games and creating a healthy environment, couples can build and maintain a healthy and fulfilling relationship.

7. Challenges couples face

Introduction:

Relationships are an essential part of human life, and love plays a significant role in nurturing these connections. However, finding and sustaining love can be challenging, as various factors come into play. Couples face different challenges in their quest for love, including cultural, societal, and individual obstacles. In this paper, we will explore some of the challenges that couples face in finding and sustaining love and provide possible solutions to these issues.

Challenges in Finding Love:

1. Social Pressure and Expectations:

One of the biggest challenges that couples face in finding love is societal pressure and expectations. Society, family, and friends often have certain expectations about when and who an individual should love. Many people feel pressure to conform to such expectations, which can lead to feelings of loneliness and isolation. For instance, in some cultures, individuals are expected to marry within their tribe, religion, or social status, making it difficult for them to pursue relationships with people outside their circles.

Solution: Couples can overcome social pressure and expectations by choosing to focus on what they truly want in a relationship rather than what others expect from them. They should prioritize their personal values, desires, and beliefs rather than external pressures. Seeking guidance from a therapist or counselor can also help individuals navigate societal pressure and expectations.

2. Online Dating Challenges:

Online dating has become increasingly popular in recent years, making it easier for people to connect with potential partners. However, it also poses a series of challenges, including fake profiles, catfishing, and misinformation. With so many options available, it can be difficult for couples to find genuine connections.

Solution: Couples can overcome online dating challenges by being vigilant and cautious when using dating apps and websites. They should take their time to know the person they are interested in, asking relevant questions, and verifying their identity. It is also important to communicate openly and honestly about their expectations and intentions to avoid misunderstandings.

3. Fear of Rejection:

Fear of rejection is a common challenge that many couples face when pursuing a romantic relationship. This fear can often prevent individuals from expressing their feelings and pursuing their potential partners. The fear of vulnerability and rejection can lead to missed opportunities for love.

Solution: Couples can overcome the fear of rejection by working on themselves and building self-confidence. They should understand that rejection is a normal part of the dating process, and everyone faces it at some point. By learning to handle rejection, individuals can approach romantic relationships with confidence and courage, knowing that their worth is not defined by their ability to attract a partner.

Challenges in Sustaining Love:

1. Communication Issues:

Communication is a critical component of any successful relationship, and lack of communication can lead to misunderstandings, conflicts, and even breakups. Couples may struggle to communicate their feelings, needs, and expectations effectively, leading to tension and resentment.

Solution: Couples can overcome communication challenges by establishing open and honest communication channels. They should actively listen to each other, avoid interrupting, and seek clarification when necessary. Regular communication check-ins, such as daily or weekly conversations, can help couples identify potential problems early and work towards resolving them.

2. Trust Issues:

Trust is the foundation of any successful relationship, and it can be challenging to maintain for couples who have experienced betrayal or infidelity. Trust issues can lead to jealousy, insecurity, and even breakups if not addressed early.

Solution: Couples can overcome trust issues by seeking the assistance of a therapist or counselor. A professional can help both parties understand the root cause of their trust issues and provide practical solutions for rebuilding trust. Couples can also commit to being transparent, honest, and accountable for their actions, and work towards establishing a sense of security in the relationship.

3. Monotony and Boredom:

Long-term relationships can sometimes become monotonous and dull, leading to a lack of excitement and passion. Couples may struggle to find new ways to keep their relationships fresh and exciting, leading to less intimacy, dissatisfaction, and even breakups.

Solution: Couples can overcome monotony and boredom by adopting new and exciting activities together. They can explore new hobbies, interests, and travel destinations, and even try new approaches to intimacy and romance. Investing in each other's personal growth and nurturing individual passions can also help couples maintain a sense of excitement and adventure in their relationship.

Conclusion:

Finding and sustaining love is not an easy task, and couples face a range of challenges along the way. However, by being aware of these obstacles and adopting practical solutions, couples can overcome them and create healthy, satisfying relationships. Overcoming social pressure, being vigilant and cautious when using dating apps, building self-confidence, establishing open communication channels, rebuilding trust, exciting new activities, and nurturing individual passions are some ways couples can overcome the challenges they face in finding and sustaining love. By striving to overcome these challenges together, couples can create a strong foundation for a lifelong relationship.

8. New couples vs experienced couples

Introduction

Love is a complicated aspect of human life. Finding and maintaining true love is the dream of every individual. However, couples with different levels of relationship experience perceive love differently. New couples always look forward to the excitement of discovering new things about each other, while experienced couples are focused on maintaining the love they have established. This paper compares new couples and experienced couples in relation to finding and sustaining love.

New Couples

New couples are individuals in a fresh and budding relationship. This means that they are still learning and discovering new things about each other. One of the attributes of new couples is that they are always excited about spending time together. They are not yet familiar with each other's faults and weaknesses. They are always willing to try new things and venture outside of their comfort zones to impress each other. New couples are always eager to get to know each other on a deeper level. They spend time exploring and asking questions about each other.

New couples are in a stage of exploration, which makes them vulnerable to making mistakes. For instance, they might be too impressed with each other at the beginning of the relationship to notice the distinct red flags. This also makes them more likely to engage in risky behavior like ignoring the importance of honesty and communication.

Another challenge new couples face is that they tend to be more emotionally dependent. Since they are still in the process of bonding, they might have a hard time handling the relationship if their partner has to be away for a few days. They also tend to become possessive over one another, which can lead to insecurity and jealousy.

To build a strong foundation for a long-lasting relationship, new couples should focus on trust and communication. They should be open with each other and strive to build a strong emotional connection. New couples should take the time to get to know each other on a deeper level. They should also be willing to compromise and find a balance between their opposing views.

Experienced Couples

Experienced couples are those that have been in a relationship for a considerable amount of time. They have gone through the excitement and passion phase of the relationship and are more focused on stability and commitment. Experienced couples have learned what works in their relationship and what doesn't. They have had enough time to understand each other's strengths and weaknesses, likes and dislikes, and have learned how to communicate with each other with ease.

The primary goal of experienced couples is to maintain the love they have established. They are more focused on building a lasting and intimate relationship. Experienced couples have learned how to handle their differences and have found a way to make it work. They have learned how to be more mindful of each other and have mastered the art of compromise.

However, experienced couples also face a set of challenges unique to their relationship stage. One of them is complacency. Some couples can become too comfortable in their relationship and start taking each other for granted. This can lead to boredom and lack of excitement, which can negatively affect the relationship. Additionally, experienced couples may become too set in their ways. For example, they may have established patterns of communication that are no longer effective but are afraid to find alternative ways to communicate.

To sustain their love over time, experienced couples should focus on maintaining their emotional connection. They should work towards creating new memories and strengthening their bond. Experienced couples should keep the element of excitement in their relationship by trying out new things together. They should be open to exploring new territories and engage in activities that both partners enjoy. Additionally, experienced couples should prioritize open communication and keep each other informed of changes in their lives.

Differences Between New Couples and Experienced Couples

There are several differences between new couples and experienced couples when it comes to finding and sustaining love. One difference is their level of emotional maturity. While new couples may be more emotionally dependent, experienced couples have already learned how to handle their differences and are more emotionally stable.

Another difference is the level of excitement they have in their relationship. New couples are often in the stage of exploring and trying new things together. They are more excited about spending time with each other, while experienced couples have already explored those possibilities. While experienced couples may not have the same level of excitement and passion as new couples, they have a deeper level of love and connection.

Communication is also a significant difference between new and experienced couples. New couples are still learning how to communicate with one another and may need more guidance to express their feelings. Experienced couples have already established effective communication in their relationship. They understand each other, and they know how to communicate effectively.

Lastly, the level of trust is another difference between new and experienced couples. New couples are still in the process of building trust. They are not yet sure of each other and may take more time to trust each other. Experienced couples have already established trust in their relationship. They know each other's strengths and weaknesses, and they have learned how to rely on each other.

Conclusion

In conclusion, love is a complex aspect of human life, and finding and sustaining love can be challenging. New couples and experienced couples perceive love differently based on their level of relationship experience. New couples are more excited about exploring and discovering new things about each other, while experienced couples are more focused on maintaining and strengthening the love they have established. The key to finding and sustaining love is to build a strong emotional connection with your partner based on trust, communication, and openness. Additionally, couples should work towards creating new memories, exploring new territories, and always keeping the element of excitement alive in their relationship to maintain a long-lasting and intimate bond.

9. Quiz

1. How can you build trust in a relationship?
   a) Being honest
   b) Keeping secrets
   c) Lying

2. What is one key to sustaining love?
   a) Consistent communication
   b) Ignoring your partner
   c) Spending less time together

3. How can you deepen your emotional connection with your partner?
   a) Discussing your feelings
   b) Avoiding talking about emotions
   c) Criticizing your partner

4. How can you show love to your partner?
   a) Doing kind gestures
   b) Ignoring their needs
   c) Being selfish

5. What is one way to maintain a healthy relationship?
   a) Compromising
   b) Being unyielding
   c) Being controlling

6. How can you keep your relationship fresh and exciting?
   a) Trying new activities together
   b) Sticking to the same routine
   c) Avoiding spending time together

7. What is one way to avoid conflicts in a relationship?
   a) Listening actively
   b) Talking over your partner
   c) Using hurtful language

8. How can you maintain respect in a relationship?
   a) Treating your partner with kindness
   b) Disrespecting your partner
   c) Being rude

9. What is one way to show commitment to your partner?
   a) Being reliable
   b) Being unreliable
   c) Not keeping your promises

10. How can you maintain intimacy in a long-term relationship?
    a) Being affectionate
    b) Being distant
    c) Ignoring your partner's needs.

IV. Sustaining Love

1. Relationship maintenance

Introduction

Love is one of the most important aspects of life. Many people strive to find love, build relationships, and maintain them. However, finding and sustaining love is not always easy. It requires effort, commitment, and dedication to build and maintain a healthy and lasting relationship. Relationship maintenance is an essential aspect of finding and sustaining love. This paper will explore what relationship maintenance is, why it is important in building a healthy relationship, the different types of relationship maintenance strategies, and how they can help in sustaining love.

What is relationship maintenance?

Relationship maintenance refers to the actions or behaviors that individuals engage in to preserve and enhance their romantic relationships. It involves the effort and dedication that individuals put into their relationships to ensure that they remain strong and healthy. Relationship maintenance goes beyond the initial attraction and falling in love. It is a continuous process of nurturing the relationship, ensuring that both partners' needs are met, and preventing conflicts and problems. Relationship maintenance is crucial in building and sustaining long-lasting love and healthy relationships.

Why is relationship maintenance important in building a healthy relationship?

Relationship maintenance is essential in building a healthy and lasting relationship. It helps to prevent conflicts and disagreements between partners. When individuals put effort into maintaining their relationships, they are more likely to understand each other's needs and develop strong communication skills. Engaging in relationship maintenance activities helps to keep the relationship fresh, exciting, and enjoyable. It creates an environment of trust and respect between partners, which provides a strong foundation for the relationship. Relationship maintenance helps to avoid the pitfalls that can lead to the end of a relationship, such as lack of communication, misunderstandings, and neglect.

Types of Relationship Maintenance Strategies

Relationship maintenance strategies can be divided into two categories: proactive and reactive. Proactive strategies involve actions that individuals take to prevent problems from happening in their relationships. Reactive strategies, on the other hand, are used to address problems that have already occurred, such as conflicts and disagreements.

Proactive Relationship Maintenance Strategies

Proactive relationship maintenance strategies involve actions that individuals take to prevent problems from happening in their relationships. They include:

1. Communication - Communication is essential in any relationship. Individuals should make an effort to talk to their partners regularly and openly. This includes discussing their feelings, needs, and expectations. Communication helps to prevent misunderstandings and conflicts, which can lead to the end of a relationship.

2. Showing appreciation - Partners should appreciate each other regularly. This involves complimenting each other's efforts, acknowledging their achievements, and expressing gratitude. Showing appreciation helps to build a positive and healthy relationship, which provides a solid foundation for love to grow.

3. Spending quality time together - Spending quality time together is essential in maintaining a healthy relationship. It involves setting aside time to be with each other, doing things that both partners enjoy. This helps to create a bond between partners, which strengthens their relationship.

4. Setting goals and working towards them - Setting goals and working towards them as a couple is an effective way to maintain a healthy relationship. It helps to create a sense of direction and purpose for the relationship, which keeps it fresh and exciting.

5. Trust - Trust is the foundation of any healthy relationship. Individuals should make an effort to build trust by being reliable, supportive, and honest. Trust helps to create a strong and secure relationship, which allows for love to thrive.

Reactive Relationship Maintenance Strategies

Reactive relationship maintenance strategies involve actions that individuals take to address problems that have already occurred, such as conflicts and disagreements. They include:

1. Active listening - Active listening involves actively paying attention to what the partner is saying. This involves responding appropriately and showing empathy. Active listening helps to prevent misunderstandings, which can lead to conflicts in the relationship.

2. Problem-solving - Individuals should work together to find solutions to problems that arise in the relationship. This involves identifying the problem, discussing possible solutions, and working together to implement the best solution.

3. Apologizing - Apologizing is an effective way to address conflicts and disagreements in the relationship. It involves taking responsibility for one's actions and expressing remorse. Apologizing helps to maintain a positive and healthy relationship, which provides a strong foundation for love to thrive.

4. Forgiveness - Forgiveness involves letting go of past hurt and resentments. It helps to restore trust and creates a positive and healthy relationship. Forgiveness allows for love to thrive and for the relationship to grow and develop.

5. Compromise - Individuals should be willing to compromise in the relationship. This involves making concessions for the partner and working towards a solution that both partners can agree on.

How relationship maintenance strategies can help in sustaining love

Relationship maintenance strategies play a crucial role in sustaining love. They help to prevent conflicts and misunderstandings, thereby creating a positive and healthy relationship. When individuals engage in relationship maintenance activities, they are more likely to understand each other's needs and develop strong communication skills. This allows for a strong foundation for the relationship to grow and develop.

In addition, relationship maintenance strategies help to keep the relationship fresh and exciting. By spending quality time together, setting goals and working towards them, and showing appreciation, partners can create a bond that strengthens the relationship and keeps it exciting.

Relationship maintenance strategies also help to prevent the pitfalls that can lead to the end of a relationship. By being proactive and addressing problems when they arise, individuals can prevent conflicts from escalating and causing irreparable damage to the relationship. This allows for the relationship to grow and develop, and for love to thrive.

Conclusion

Relationship maintenance is an essential aspect of finding and sustaining love. It involves the effort and dedication that individuals put into their relationships to ensure that they remain strong and healthy. Relationship maintenance strategies can be divided into two categories: proactive and reactive. Proactive strategies involve actions that individuals take to prevent problems from happening in their relationships, while reactive strategies are used to address problems that have already occurred. By engaging in relationship maintenance activities, individuals can create a positive and healthy relationship that provides a strong foundation for love to thrive.

2. Keeping the spark alive

Introduction:

Love is an extraordinary feeling that connects two individuals and fills them with joy, happiness, and satisfaction. Falling in love is relatively easy; however, keeping the spark alive throughout the relationship is the challenging task. Every relationship goes through ups and downs, but how couples deal with them determines the success or failure of the relationship. In this essay, we will discuss how to find love and sustain it, focusing on how couples can keep the spark alive in their relationships.

Finding Love:

Finding love is not always easy and straightforward. Some people find love through chance encounters, while others use dating apps and sites to meet their partners. Whatever the case, finding love requires effort, patience, and a willingness to take risks. Here are some tips for finding love:

1. Define what you want: Before you start searching for a partner, you need to define what you want in a relationship. What are your deal breakers? What are your must-haves? Knowing what you want will help you narrow down your search and increase your chances of finding someone who is right for you.

2. Be open-minded: Sometimes, we have a set idea of what our ideal partner should be like, and this can limit our options. Being open-minded and flexible can help you find someone who is not your usual "type" but who may turn out to be the perfect match for you.

3. Use online dating sites: Online dating has become increasingly popular in recent years, and it is an excellent way to meet new people. However, you need to be cautious and choose reputable dating sites to ensure your safety.

4. Join social groups and activities: Joining social groups and activities can help you socialize and meet new people. It also provides an opportunity to connect with like-minded individuals who share your interests.

Sustaining Love:

Once you find love, the next challenge is to sustain it. Relationships take effort, and both partners must be willing to work together to keep the spark alive. Here are some tips for sustaining love:

1. Communication: Communication is vital in any relationship. It is essential to talk openly and honestly about your feelings, needs, and desires. Communication helps to build trust and strengthens the bond between partners.

2. Quality Time: Spending quality time together is essential for maintaining the spark in a relationship. This can be as simple as having dinner together, going for a walk, or doing a fun activity together.

3. Show Appreciation: It is crucial to show appreciation for your partner. Expressing gratitude and saying thank you can go a long way in making your partner feel valued and loved.

4. Compromise: Relationships require compromise. Both partners must be willing to compromise and make sacrifices for the benefit of the relationship.

5. Keep things exciting: Keeping things exciting in a relationship is essential for maintaining the spark. This can be done by trying new things together, going on adventures, or surprising your partner with a thoughtful gesture.

Keeping the Spark Alive:

Keeping the spark alive is essential for the success and longevity of a relationship. Here are some tips for keeping the spark alive:

1. Date Nights: Setting aside regular date nights is a fun way to keep the spark alive. It provides an opportunity to spend quality time together and do something special.

2. Show Affection: Showing affection is essential in a relationship. Small gestures such as holding hands, hugging, and kissing can go a long way in maintaining the spark.

3. Compliment Each Other: Complimenting each other is an excellent way to boost the spark in a relationship. Saying kind words and showing appreciation can make your partner feel loved and valued.

4. Keep the Romance Alive: Romance is an essential aspect of any relationship. Doing small things such as leaving love notes, surprising your partner with a thoughtful gesture, or planning a surprise weekend getaway can keep the romance alive.

5. Take Care of Yourself: Taking care of yourself is vital in keeping the spark alive. When you feel good about yourself, you are more confident, and your partner will find you more attractive.

Conclusion:

In conclusion, finding and sustaining love requires effort, patience, and a willingness to take risks. Communication, spending quality time together, showing appreciation, compromise, and keeping things exciting are all essential for maintaining the spark in a relationship. By following these tips, couples can ensure that their relationships are strong, healthy, and fulfilling. Remember, the key to keeping the spark alive is to never stop trying and never take your partner for granted.

3. Supporting each other's growth and development

Introduction:

When it comes to finding and sustaining love, there is no magic formula or rational method to follow. Relationships are not fixed or scripted instances because every human being is different. However, one of the most crucial ingredients in any successful relationship is the willingness of both partners to support each other's growth and development. This support can come in many forms, from encouraging each other to achieve their goals to offering emotional and physical comfort in tough times. The purpose of this essay is to examine different ways partners can support each other's growth and development in order to find and sustain love.

Create a Safe and Supportive Environment:

Creating a safe and supportive environment is one of the most effective ways to find and sustain love. A supportive and nurturing atmosphere allows partners to express their emotions and communicate their needs without the fear of being judged or rejected. This environment will be built through sharing experiences and challenges with each other and collaboratively working on a positive future. In doing so, both partners will have a greater understanding of each other's nature and goals, which is an excellent foundation on which to build a genuinely loving relationship.

Encourage Each Other's Goals:

Encouraging each other's goals is crucial to supporting each other's growth and development. In a relationship, it is important to support and be an advocate for your partner's dreams and ambitions in both their personal and professional life. This support will be invaluable when it comes to achieving goals, despite challenges and difficulties. A good partner will listen to the needs and dreams of the other person and offer real, heartfelt support in return.

Maintain a Sense of Independence:

Independence in a relationship is essential to establishing a supportive and balanced atmosphere. It is important for both partners to have their own interests, passions, and friends that they don't share as a couple. As individuals, each person will have unique perspectives on various things, which can make for interesting conversations within the relationship. Supporting each other's independence will also allow space for personal self-growth, which is essential for sustainability in a relationship.

Communicate Effectively:

Effective communication is fundamental to supporting each other's growth and development in a relationship. It is not always easy to communicate effectively, but learning to listen and express yourself honestly with your partner will allow you to learn and grow as individuals. When you are fully engaged in conversations with each other, you can avoid misunderstandings that may arise in communication and work collaboratively to remedy any situation. Communication does not come easily for everyone, but even small steps to improve the way you communicate with each other will help to solidify your connection.

Be Supportive During Hard Times:

Supporting each other through difficult times is one of the most important aspects of a loving relationship. Tough times can force people to feel vulnerable and hopeless. Whenever your partner is struggling or going through a hard period emotionally, it's your responsibility to offer comfort, love, and understanding. Helping your partner recognize they're not alone in their struggle and reminding them of their strengths and capabilities can provide the motivation they need. Supporting your partner through difficult times helps to forge a closer bond between the two of you. Together, you can find the help and resources necessary to work through anything.

Conclusion:

Ultimately, supporting each other's growth and development in a relationship requires a mindset of focus from both partners. It is about acknowledging and supporting each other's strengths and weaknesses, empathizing with each other's emotions and working collaboratively to redefine who you are as individuals and as a couple. This kind of support is essential when it comes to finding and sustaining a loving relationship. The ideas highlighted in this essay are only a few of the ways in which partners can support each other's growth and development. However, one thing is clear, the more partners can find ways to support one another, the stronger and more fulfilling their love will be.

4. Overcoming obstacles and challenges

Introduction

Love is a complex emotion that is both essential for human existence and fraught with obstacles and challenges. Many individuals struggle to find and sustain love due to personal and societal factors that can create barriers to emotional connection. Overcoming these obstacles and challenges is critical to building and maintaining fulfilling relationships. In this paper, we will explore several of the common obstacles and challenges individuals may face when trying to find and sustain love, and provide strategies for overcoming these barriers.

1. Fear of Vulnerability

One of the primary obstacles to finding and sustaining love is a fear of vulnerability. Many individuals are hesitant to open themselves up emotionally out of fear of rejection or abandonment. This fear can cause people to avoid love altogether or to hold back in their relationships, ultimately preventing them from fully connecting with their partners.

To overcome this obstacle, individuals must begin by recognizing and accepting their fear of vulnerability. It is essential to understand that this fear is a natural response to the potential risks of emotionally connecting with another person. However, it is important not to let this fear dictate your actions. Instead, work on developing a sense of emotional resilience by acknowledging and responding positively to your emotions. Furthermore, it is essential to communicate openly and honestly with your partner about your feelings and concerns, creating a safe space for vulnerability and emotional connection.

2. Fear of Intimacy

Another common obstacle to finding and sustaining love is a fear of intimacy. This fear is often related to the fear of vulnerability but can take different forms. For some individuals, fear of intimacy manifests as a fear of physical intimacy, which can prevent them from engaging in sexual or physical contact with their partners. For others, fear of intimacy manifests as a fear of emotional intimacy, making it challenging to build deep emotional connections with others.

Overcoming fear of intimacy requires taking small steps towards building intimacy, both physical and emotional. Individuals struggling with physical intimacy may benefit from gradually exploring physical contact with their partners, starting with non-sexual touch and building towards more intimate contact. Those with a fear of emotional intimacy may benefit from opening up about their feelings gradually, starting with small disclosures and building towards deeper emotional connections over time. Ultimately, overcoming fear of intimacy requires a commitment to being open and vulnerable in your relationships.

3. Poor Self-Image

Individuals with low self-esteem may struggle to find and sustain love, often believing that they are unworthy of love or incapable of building fulfilling relationships. This negative self-image can become a self-fulfilling prophecy, as it can lead individuals to settle for less than they deserve in their relationships or to sabotage their connections out of a belief that they are not deserving of love.

To overcome this obstacle, individuals must work on building their self-esteem and recognizing their own worth. This can involve working with a therapist, practicing self-compassion, and re-framing negative self-talk. Furthermore, individuals must learn to set boundaries and communicate their needs in their relationships, recognizing that they are worthy of love and deserving of a partner who respects and values them.

4. Difficulty Trusting

Trust is a critical component of any healthy relationship, but it can be challenging to cultivate when individuals have experienced past hurts or disappointments in their relationships. Difficulty trusting can manifest in a variety of ways, from jealousy and possessiveness to avoiding emotional vulnerability altogether.

To overcome this obstacle, individuals must work on building trust in themselves and their partners. This may involve seeking therapy to process past hurts and traumas, practicing effective communication, and gradually building trust through small, committed acts of vulnerability and honesty. Furthermore, it is essential to set clear boundaries and expectations in your relationships, creating a safe environment for emotional connection and openness.

5. Incompatible Goals and Values

One of the most significant challenges to sustaining love is when individuals have incompatible goals and values. This can lead to disagreements and conflict, ultimately preventing the relationship from moving forward.

To overcome this challenge, it is essential to prioritize open and honest communication from the beginning of the relationship. Individuals must be clear about their goals and values, asking questions and actively listening to their partners' perspectives. If goals and values are too divergent to reconcile, it may be necessary to re-evaluate the relationship and consider whether it is ultimately compatible and sustainable.

6. External Pressures

In addition to personal obstacles, individuals may face external pressures that can make it challenging to find and sustain love. These pressures may include cultural expectations, family pressures, or societal norms that can create barriers to emotional connection and fulfillment.

To overcome external pressures, individuals must be intentional about creating boundaries and establishing their own values and goals for their relationships. This may involve seeking support from friends or family members who understand and respect their values, being willing to challenge cultural norms that do not align with their priorities, and considering alternative relationship models or lifestyles that better match their goals and values. Ultimately, it is essential to remain true to oneself and prioritize one's own emotional fulfillment and well-being.

Conclusion

Finding and sustaining love can be challenging, particularly when individuals face personal and external obstacles that can make it challenging to connect and build fulfilling relationships. However, by recognizing and addressing these obstacles head-on, individuals can overcome these challenges and build strong and sustainable connections with their partners. Whether it requires developing emotional resilience, challenging negative self-talk, or breaking free of external pressures, the key to finding and sustaining love is a commitment to authenticity, honesty, and vulnerability in our relationships.

References:

Burley, T. (2018). The fear of vulnerability: Overcoming the obstacles to emotional connection. Retrieved from https://www.psychologytoday.com/us/blog/ the-rediscovery-manhood/201811/the-fear-vulnerability

Gupta, S. (2018). Overcoming fear of intimacy in romantic relationships. Retrieved from https://positivepsychology.com/ fear-of-intimacy/

Young, E. (2017). 5 ways to overcome trust issues in your relationship. Retrieved from https://www.bustle.com/p/5-ways-to-overcome-trust-issues-in-your-relationship-55469.

5. Dealing with issues of infidelity and betrayal

Introduction

Infidelity and betrayal are some of the most challenging issues that a couple can face in their relationship. They can cause significant emotional distress and pain to the individuals involved, and give rise to feelings of mistrust, anger, and disappointment. However, with the right tools, it is possible to overcome these difficulties and rebuild a stronger, healthier relationship. In this paper, I will be discussing how to deal with issues of infidelity and betrayal in the context of finding and sustaining love.

Understanding Infidelity and Betrayal

Infidelity occurs when one partner engages in a sexual or emotional relationship with someone outside their primary relationship. Betrayal, on the other hand, can occur in various ways, such as lies, deception, breaking promises, hiding information, and not being emotionally present in the relationship. Both infidelity and betrayal can cause damage to the trust and emotional safety in a relationship.

Infidelity and betrayal can occur for different reasons. Some common reasons for infidelity include a lack of emotional connection, dissatisfaction with the current relationship, intimacy issues, an opportunity to cheat, poor communication, and a lack of commitment to the relationship. Betrayal can arise from a partner's fear of confrontation or criticism, a desire to protect themselves, a lack of trust in their partner, or simply a lack of concern for their partner's feelings.

When infidelity and betrayal occur, it can lead to a range of reactions, including feelings of anger, sadness, hurt, and disbelief. However, it is important to understand that these reactions are normal and natural, and they do not define the individual's worth or value.

Dealing With Infidelity and Betrayal

Facing infidelity and betrayal can be difficult, but there are steps that couples can take to move forward and overcome these challenges. Here are some of the ways that couples can deal with infidelity and betrayal:

1. Be Honest

The first step in overcoming infidelity and betrayal is to be honest with your partner. This means admitting to any wrongdoing and being open and transparent about your feelings, thoughts, and actions. Honesty is crucial in rebuilding trust and repairing the damaged relationship.

2. Practice Active Listening

Active listening is an important skill in any relationship, but it is especially crucial in times of crisis. To practice active listening, turn off all distractions, give your full attention to your partner, and try to understand their perspective without judgment. This will help you to communicate better and show your partner that you care about their feelings.

3. Seek Professional Help

It can be challenging to deal with infidelity and betrayal on your own, and seeking professional help can be a crucial step in moving forward. A licensed therapist can provide guidance, support, and a safe space for open and honest communication.

4. Take Time for Yourself

When dealing with infidelity and betrayal, it can be easy to focus solely on the relationship and forget about your own needs and well-being. Taking time for yourself, whether it's engaging in self-care activities or pursuing personal interests, can help you to re-center and find balance in your life.

Finding Love After Infidelity and Betrayal

Finding love after infidelity and betrayal can be challenging, but it is possible. Here are some tips for finding and sustaining healthy, fulfilling relationships:

1. Know Yourself

Before entering any new relationship, it is important to know yourself and your personal values and goals. This will help you to find a partner who shares your values and supports your goals.

2. Take It Slow

It can be tempting to jump into a new relationship immediately after experiencing infidelity and betrayal, but taking it slow can be beneficial. This gives you time to heal, reflect, and ensure that you are ready for a new relationship.

3. Communicate Openly

Clear, honest communication is key to any successful relationship. Practice active listening, express yourself honestly, and work with your partner to build trust and understanding.

4. Set Boundaries

Setting boundaries is important in any relationship, but it is especially crucial after experiencing infidelity and betrayal. Clearly communicating your needs and expectations can help to create a safe and healthy relationship.

Conclusion

Infidelity and betrayal are challenging issues that can cause significant emotional pain and distress. However, with the right tools and resources, it is possible to overcome these difficulties and find and sustain love in healthy, fulfilling relationships. By being honest, practicing active listening, seeking professional help, and taking time for yourself, you can overcome difficult times and create a strong, supportive relationship that will stand the test of time.

6. Quiz

1. What is one way to sustain love in a relationship?
    a. Spend all your free time together
    b. Ignore your partner's needs and focus on your own
    c. Communicate openly and honestly with your partner
    d. Keep secrets from your partner

2. What can help sustain love in a long-term relationship?
    a. Having identical interests and hobbies
    b. Spending every moment together
    c. Giving each other space and independence
    d. Ignoring each other's feelings and emotions

3. How can couples maintain intimacy in a long-term relationship?
    a. Ignoring each other's emotional needs
    b. Changing themselves to please their partner
    c. Allowing space and independence
    d. Regularly expressing love, affection, and appreciation

4. What is a key factor in sustaining love?
    a. Ignoring your partner's needs and desires
    b. Trying to change your partner to fit your ideal image
    c. Striving for open and honest communication
    d. All of the above

5. How can criticism damage a long-term relationship?

a. It can lead to a lack of trust and respect
b. It can improve communication and understanding
c. It can increase mutual appreciation and support
d. It has no effect on the relationship.

Answers: 1.c 2.c 3.d 4.c 5.a

V. Common Issues

1. Communication problems

Page 1: Introduction to Communication Problems in Relationships

Communication is vital to any successful relationship. It is the foundation for understanding one another's needs, desires, and perspectives. Communication can make or break a relationship, and it is especially crucial when it comes to finding and sustaining love. In this essay, we will discuss the communication problems that can arise in relationships and their impact on how people find and sustain love.

Page 2: Communication Problems and Finding Love

One of the biggest communication problems that people face when trying to find love is miscommunication. Miscommunication can lead to misunderstandings, hurt feelings, and even breakups. When two people are trying to get to know each other, it is essential that they are clear and concise in their communication. This means actively listening, asking questions, and being open and honest. When these elements are missing, the chances of finding love diminish greatly.

Another communication problem that can arise when trying to find love is the fear of rejection. People often hold back or withhold their feelings because they are afraid of being rejected. This fear can prevent individuals from expressing their true selves and hinder the ability to connect with others on a deeper level. Overcoming the fear of rejection requires one to acknowledge their feelings, communicate them effectively, and be open to vulnerability.

Page 3: Communication Problems and Sustaining Love

Communication problems don't just disappear once people have found love. They can persist and even worsen over time. The longer a couple is together, the more likely they are to experience conflicts that stem from miscommunication. One of the most significant challenges that couples face in sustaining love is communicating effectively during conflict.

Communication during a disagreement can become heated and make matters worse if one or both parties shut down, interrupt, or become defensive. Instead, it is crucial to remain calm, listen actively, and practice empathy. Empathy is the ability to understand and share the feelings of another. When both individuals in a relationship can practice empathy, they can communicate their needs and feelings more effectively.

Page 4: Common Communication Problems in Relationships
There are several common communication problems that couples face in relationships. One is blaming and accusing. When one partner blames the other for something, it can create a defensive reaction, which leads to a breakdown in communication. It is essential to discuss issues without blaming the other person and instead take responsibility for one's own actions.

Another common communication problem is lack of active listening. Active listening involves not only hearing what the other person is saying but also understanding their perspective and validating their feelings. When one partner interrupts or dismisses the other's point of view, communication breaks down, and feelings of frustration and resentment can build.

Page 5: How to Improve Communication in Relationships

Improving communication in relationships takes effort and practice. It requires both individuals to be willing to listen, learn, and grow. One way to improve communication is to practice active listening. This means being present in the conversation and giving the other person your undivided attention. It also involves asking questions to gain a better understanding of their perspective.

Another way to improve communication is to avoid making assumptions. Assumptions can lead to misunderstandings and hurt feelings. Instead, it is essential to clarify information and ask questions when unsure. Being transparent and honest about one's feelings and intentions can also help improve communication in a relationship.

Page 6: Conclusion

Communication is an essential component of finding and sustaining love. Miscommunication can lead to misunderstandings, hurt feelings, and even breakups. When two people are trying to get to know each other, it is important that they communicate effectively and be open and honest. Similarly, communication problems can persist in a relationship and even worsen over time, impacting the ability to sustain love. Overcoming communication problems requires active listening, empathy, and a willingness to learn and grow. By communicating effectively, couples can deepen their connection and foster a healthy and lasting love.

2. Trust issues

Abstract

Trust is an essential element in every relationship, particularly romantic relationships. Trust issues have been a major problem in relationships, which has caused many breakups and heartbreaks. Finding and sustaining a healthy and lasting relationship requires trust. This paper will discuss the concept of trust issues and how it relates to finding and sustaining love.

Introduction

Humans are social beings who crave love and connection. Romantic relationships help provide these needs, and trust is one of the crucial components of forming and maintaining intimate relationships. Trust is an essential part of creating stable and healthy relationships and a crucial component in sustaining love. The absence of trust can cause severe damage to relationships, leading to breakups, mistrust, and heartbreaks. This paper aims to discuss trust issues in romantic relationships and how to find and sustain love amidst trust issues.

Trust Issues in Relationships

Trust issues mainly arise from a past experience of betrayal, infidelity, or lies. A person who has been hurt before in a past experience finds it challenging to trust in a new relationship. Trust issues can manifest in different ways, such as fear of being cheated on, being overly suspicious, or feeling insecure in the relationship. Some relationships are established on trust issues as they struggle to overcome the lingering doubts in their minds based on their past experiences.

Trust is vital for any relationship, and if it is consistently undermined, the relationship becomes vulnerable. Suspicion or fear can result in jealousy, controlling or possessive behavior, or insecurity. Trust issues can be inculcated in people through different life experiences. Some people have been betrayed by their friends, family members, or ex-partners, leading to an innate mistrust. Lack of trust in a relationship can result in severe emotional trauma. Such traumas can result in a profound sense of loss, a loss of self-esteem, or a loss of self-worth.

Trust is necessary for relationships to thrive. Without trust, people struggle to express emotions, fears, and vulnerabilities, and they shut down. Trust allows people to be genuine and honest. It is the bedrock of intimacy in romantic relationships.

Finding Love Amidst Trust Issues

In the quest for finding love, people need to understand that trust is a necessary component. Without trust, relationships will struggle to flourish. The question arises; how can a person find love amidst trust issues? First, they must understand that every new relationship is unique and must be treated differently. It is best not to go into a new relationship with the same fears and insecurities from previous relationships. It's crucial to recognize the influence of previous experiences on relationship fears and a willingness to address those fears.

When looking for love in a new relationship, one must take their time to learn about the other person. Establishing trust in a new relationship takes time. People should always be cautious when getting into a new relationship, particularly if they have had trust issues in the past. It's important to convey your fears and concerns to your partner. By doing so, it gives your partner a chance to earn your trust and address those fears.

People with trust issues should learn to communicate effectively. Communicating allows people to express their fears and insecurities, which helps foster a healthy relationship. When communicating, it's important to be open, honest, and non-judgmental, as it promotes trust in the relationship.

Set boundaries and reasonable expectations in the relationship and do not neglect them. Setting boundaries involves being clear on what you expect from the relationship and what is unacceptable. It ensures that your partner respects them. If those boundaries are crossed, it is important to communicate what they are and why it is important not to compromise with them.

In a relationship, it is important to give not only love but also trust. Trust is seen as a gift. To trust someone, one must give them the right to disappoint, and if they come through, the relationship will be strengthened. Trust is built when people can open up and show their vulnerabilities, and when they do not continue to carry their fears from the past.

Sustaining Love Amidst Trust Issues

Trust issues can threaten even the most loving and healthy relationships. When trust is betrayed, the impact can be significant, and rebuilding trust is not always easy. Sustaining love amidst trust issues requires both partners to work together to build and maintain trust. As the relationship progresses, it's crucial to continue to earn each other's trust.

Trust is the foundation of a lasting and healthy relationship. Building trust is not a one-time occurrence; it requires consistent effort and action. To sustain love amidst trust issues, both partners need to be open and honest in their communication. Effective communication is a significant part of building trust. People should always be willing to listen and be empathetic to their partner's concerns.

In a relationship, respect plays a significant role in building and maintaining trust. Respect involves being mindful of each other's feelings, privacy, and boundaries. Understanding each other's boundaries is crucial to building trust in a relationship. When boundaries are crossed, it can cause significant harm and distrust.

To sustain love amidst trust issues, it is essential to keep the romance alive. Romance keeps the relationship healthy and brings couples closer. Dedicating time for each other, creating new experiences, and engaging in new activities together is an effective way to keep the fire burning.

Lastly, both partners must be willing to forgive. Forgiveness is crucial in sustaining love amidst trust issues. Every relationship will encounter challenges, and being able to forgive each other when there are mistakes is an important part of building trust in a relationship. Forgiveness can help heal past traumas, bring couples closer, and build stronger bonds.

Conclusion

Trust issues are a significant problem in relationships. It stems from past betrayal, infidelity, or lies in previous relationships. Finding and sustaining love amidst trust issues requires effective communication, setting boundaries, and building respect in the relationship. Trust is a crucial component of any relationship. It is essential to establish and maintain trust in a healthy and long-lasting relationship. To sustain love amidst trust issues, both partners must be willing to work together to build and maintain trust and be willing to forgive when there are mistakes. Ultimately, if both partners are committed to making the relationship work, trust can be restored, and love can thrive.

3. Conflict resolution problems

Conflict resolution is a crucial aspect of every romantic relationship. Disagreements and disputes are bound to arise in any given relationship; the crucial aspect is how the individuals involved in the relationship resolve them. Failure to address and resolve conflicts can lead to unending fights, arguments, and disagreements that ultimately extinguish the flame of love and affection in a romantic relationship. Learning and adopting conflict resolution strategies is, therefore, essential in finding and sustaining love. This essay explores the conflict resolution problems that affect a romantic relationship and how to find and sustain love despite these issues.

Conflicts in Romance

Romantic relationships are some of the most dynamic interactions we engage in as human beings. They include a wide range of emotions, including love, passion, and trust, but they are also ripe for discord and misunderstandings. It's hardly a surprise that conflicts can occur in even the happiest and loving relationships. In fact, infatuation and the strong emotional bond that comes with it can easily blind us to communication issues and important differences that may cause friction down the line. Common sources of conflict in romantic relationships include differences in personalities, values, needs, and wants.

Personality Differences

Disparate personalities between romantic partners can be a significant source of conflict. Every individual has unique personality characteristics, such as introversion or extroversion, and these can create friction in a romantic relationship as communication and interaction styles vary. For instance, an introverted partner may shy away from social events, while an extroverted partner may want to participate in them. In such instances, the introverted partner may perceive their partner as insensitive or selfish and create conflict in the relationship.

Value Differences

Values and beliefs are critical aspects of every human being's personality, and they affect how we perceive the world and interact with it. Values such as religion and politics can lead to significant conflicts in romantic relationships, especially if they are deeply held. For instance, if one partner insists on raising their children following a particular religious doctrine while the other partner desires to raise them with secular values and scientific outlook, significant conflicts may arise.

Needs and Wants Differences

Needs and desires differ between two individuals even within a romantic relationship. For instance, one partner may desire to settle down and start a family, while the other seeks adventure and travel. One partner may also want to focus on their career, while the other desires to prioritize starting a family. These differences in needs and desires can lead to significant conflicts in a romantic relationship if not addressed amicably.

Conflict Resolution in Romantic Relationships

Effective conflict resolution in romantic relationships is the foundation of any healthy and sustainable relationship. The conflict resolution process in a romantic relationship should involve respectful communication and negotiation, taking into account both partners' perspectives and emotions. The following are some of the effective conflict resolution strategies to adopt in a romantic relationship:

1. Communication

Communication in a romantic relationship is the key to conflict resolution. Partners must learn to communicate effectively, explicitly state their thoughts and emotions, and listen actively. Active listening means paying attention to your partner's communication without interrupting or dismissing their opinions and feelings. This helps everyone feel heard and valued.

2. Problem Solving

Learning effective problem-solving skills is essential in addressing and resolving conflicts in a romantic relationship. To solve a problem, the first step is to brainstorm a list of potential solutions. The next step is to evaluate each solution's pros and cons, assessing its feasibility and desirability. Finally, partners can decide on a mutually acceptable solution that considers both individual perspectives.

3. Compromise

Compromise is an essential aspect of conflict resolution in a romantic relationship. Partners must learn to give and take, finding common ground in their individual preferences and opinions. The goal in any conflict is not to "win" but to resolve the conflict and maintain a healthy, respectful relationship.

4. Learning from Experience

Conflict resolution should not be a one-and-done process in a romantic relationship. As partners navigate future issues and disagreements, they should assess their successes and failures in the previous conflict resolutions, evaluate what worked and what didn't, and learn from their experiences.

Sustaining and Nurturing Love

Sustaining and nurturing love in a romantic relationship is crucial to maintaining a healthy and long-lasting bond. It takes effort and commitment from both partners and involves acknowledging and respecting individual differences, committing to effective communication, and nurturing the relationship even amid conflicts. The following are some of the effective strategies to find and sustain love in a romantic relationship:

1. Self-reflection

Before finding love and beginning a romantic relationship, it's crucial to engage in self-reflection. Understanding yourself, your needs, desires, and values, is the first step in finding a compatible and fulfilling partner. Self-reflection helps decrease the potential for conflicts that arise when two individuals are not compatible on the values and needs that matter to them.

2. Mutual Respect

Mutual respect is crucial in sustaining love in a romantic relationship. Partners must acknowledge and respect each other's feelings, opinions, and perspectives, even within conflicts. Partners should strive to treat each other respectfully, without belittling or demeaning each other.

3. Open Communication

Effective and open communication is the foundation of every healthy and sustainable romantic relationship. Partners should be honest and transparent in communicating their feelings, thoughts, and perspectives, even amidst conflict.

4. Tolerance

Individual differences are bound to exist in romantic relationships, and partners should learn to tolerate these differences to sustain love. Partners should strive to find common ground and compromise on individual preferences and opinions, even when they differ.

5. Nurturing Love

Nurturing love in a romantic relationship involves consistent and intentional efforts to maintain the connection and bond between partners. Engaging in shared activities, taking vacations together, and other romantic gestures help sustain and nurture love in a romantic relationship.

Conclusion

Conflict resolution is an essential aspect of every romantic relationship. Conflicts are inevitable, and partners must learn effective conflict resolution strategies to resolve conflicts amicably. Effective conflict resolution involves effective communication, problem-solving, compromise, and learning from experiences. In sustaining love in a romantic relationship, partners must engage in self-reflection, mutual respect, open communication, tolerance, and consistent efforts to nurture the love and bond between partners. By learning and adopting these strategies, finding and sustaining love in a romantic relationship becomes a feasible and fulfilling experience.

4. Unequal distribution of responsibilities

Introduction:

Love is an essential and fundamental aspect of human life. It gives life a new meaning and happiness. Couples in love tend to enjoy every bit of life with their partners around. However, finding and sustaining love in relationships is not a walk in the park. It comes with lots of challenges, including an unequal distribution of responsibilities between partners. In most cases, women tend to bear the bulk of household chores, child-rearing responsibilities, and work-related pressures, leaving men with little or no responsibilities. This paper seeks to explore the unequal distribution of responsibilities in relationships and its impact on finding and sustaining love.

Unequal Distribution of Responsibilities:

The unequal distribution of responsibilities is a typical scenario in relationships, and it can have both negative and positive impacts on finding and sustaining love. The unequal distribution of responsibilities can lead to a power imbalance in the relationship, where one partner is more dominant than the other. This power imbalance can lead to the exploitation of one partner at the expense of the other. For instance, if one partner has all the financial responsibilities, they can misuse their power and make decisions without consulting the other partner. This can lead to a breakdown in the relationship and eventual separation.

On the other hand, the unequal distribution of responsibilities can be beneficial in a relationship if it's done voluntarily. For instance, if one partner is providing for the family financially, the other partner can take care of the household chores, child-rearing, and other domestic responsibilities. This can bring stability to the relationship and contribute to long-term happiness. However, the problem arises when one partner is forced to take up most of the responsibilities without their consent.

The Impact of Unequal Distribution of Responsibilities on Finding Love:

In most cases, the unequal distribution of responsibilities can impact the process of finding love negatively. For instance, a partner who is overly burdened with domestic responsibilities may find it hard to socialize or participate in activities that may lead to finding love. They may not have enough time and energy to commit to exploring relationships outside their current relationship. This can lead to isolation and limited opportunities to meet and interact with new people.

Moreover, the unequal distribution of responsibilities can lead to a partner who is overwhelmed with maintaining the household or raising children, feeling unappreciated and undervalued. This can lead to feelings of frustration, resentment, and distance in the relationship. Additionally, it can lead to a lack of trust and respect between partners, ultimately undermining the potential for finding love.

The Impact of Unequal Distribution of Responsibilities on Sustaining Love:

The unequal distribution of responsibilities can have a significant impact on sustaining love in a relationship. If one partner is bearing the bulk of responsibilities, it can lead to feelings of stress, fatigue, and burnout. This can affect their ability to maintain intimacy in the relationship and connect with their partner emotionally and physically. Additionally, it can lead to a lack of appreciation and acknowledgment of the efforts and sacrifices made by the other partner. This can erode the foundation of the relationship over time, leading to conflicts and eventually separation.

Furthermore, the unequal distribution of responsibilities can affect the overall quality of the relationship. A partner who is overly burdened with responsibilities may not have the time and energy to fully participate in the relationship and give the attention and care that their partner needs. This can lead to feelings of neglect and disconnection, which can ultimately lead to a breakdown in the relationship.

Addressing Unequal Distribution of Responsibilities:

Addressing the unequal distribution of responsibilities is essential in finding and sustaining love in a relationship. It requires both partners to acknowledge the existence of unequal responsibilities and work together to find a balance. It involves open and honest communication about each partner's expectations, needs, and limitations. Additionally, it requires a willingness by each partner to listen and understand the other's point of view.

One way to address the unequal distribution of responsibilities is to share responsibilities equally. Both partners should contribute to household chores, child-rearing, and work-related pressures. This can lead to a more harmonious and balanced relationship, where both partners feel valued, appreciated, and respected.

Another way to address the unequal distribution of responsibilities is to delegate responsibilities. Each partner can take up specific duties that they can handle best. For instance, if the man can comfortably handle heavy lifting, he can take care of outdoor chores, while the woman takes care of indoor chores like cooking and cleaning. This can bring a sense of order and balance to the relationship.

Partnering with a professional can also help address the unequal distribution of responsibilities. A therapist can help both partners understand the dynamics of their relationship and find ways to find a balance that works for both parties.

Conclusion:

In conclusion, the unequal distribution of responsibilities is a significant challenge in relationships. It can have both positive and negative impacts on finding and sustaining love. An unequal distribution of responsibilities can lead to power imbalances, exploitation, and disconnection in the relationship. It can also impact the process of finding love and limit opportunities to socialize and meet new people. To address this, both partners should acknowledge the unequal distribution of responsibilities and work toward finding a balance that works for both parties. It requires open communication, willingness to listen and understand, sharing or delegating responsibilities and partnering with a professional if necessary. Ultimately, finding and sustaining love requires both partners to be fully committed and invested in the relationship.

5. Differences in values or goals

Introduction

Throughout history, love has been one of the most celebrated aspects of human existence. It has been the inspiration for songs, movies, poems, and artistic expressions. However, what love means to different people varies greatly based on cultural, social, and personal values and experiences. In this essay, we will explore the differences in values and goals in relation to how to find and sustain love.

Cultural Differences

Cultural values and norms play a significant role in shaping how individuals perceive love. For instance, in Western societies such as the United States, love is often associated with romance, physical attraction, and compatibility. In contrast, in Asian cultures, such as Japan, love is often viewed as a sense of duty and responsibility towards one's partner. Therefore, the ideal partner is not necessarily someone who makes the heart race but someone who is reliable and can support the family.

Another cultural difference in how to find and sustain love is the importance of family and community support. In many African, Asian, and Middle Eastern cultures, the success of a relationship is determined by the approval and support of family and friends. Therefore, it is not just about finding the right person for oneself but also for the community. In many Western societies, however, the focus is on individual happiness and fulfillment, and the importance of family and community support varies depending on the individual's values and beliefs.

Social Differences

Social status and socioeconomic factors also influence how individuals approach finding and sustaining love. For instance, people from different socioeconomic backgrounds may have different priorities and expectations when it comes to relationships. Those from more affluent backgrounds may focus more on finding a partner who shares their social status and wealth. In contrast, individuals from a lower socioeconomic background may prioritize finding someone who is supportive and caring, regardless of financial status.

Additionally, societal expectations of gender roles and expectations can also impact how people approach relationships. In traditional gender roles, men are expected to be providers and women to be caregivers. While these roles have shifted in many societies, they still influence how individuals approach partnership and child-rearing.

Personal Differences

Lastly, personal values, experiences, and beliefs also play a significant role in how individuals approach relationships. For instance, religious beliefs can affect a person's view of love and the ideal partner. Someone with strong spiritual convictions may prioritize finding someone who shares their faith and values. Similarly, past experiences with relationships, such as divorce or infidelity, can impact a person's outlook on love and their approach to finding a partner.

Moreover, personality traits, such as introversion or extraversion, can also impact how individuals approach relationships. For instance, an introverted person may prefer a low-key relationship, while an extraverted person may enjoy more socializing and public displays of affection.

Finding and Sustaining Love

Despite the differences in values and goals when it comes to finding and sustaining love, there are some universal principles that individuals and couples can follow to find and sustain love.

Firstly, open communication is crucial for building and maintaining healthy relationships. Being honest and transparent with oneself and one's partner is essential to establish trust and deep connections. Good communication skills involve active listening, clear expression of one's thoughts and feelings, and empathy for the other person's point of view.

Secondly, mutual respect is crucial for the success of relationships. Respecting each other's boundaries, values, and opinions is essential for building lasting connections. It means working to understand different perspectives and finding common ground that supports both parties.

Thirdly, a commitment to personal growth and development is crucial. Relationships provide opportunities for personal growth and development for individuals and couples. A healthy relationship requires a willingness to learn, adapt, and compromise as individuals.

Conclusion

Although love is a significant part of what makes us human, it means different things to different people. Cultural, social, and personal differences can all impact how individuals approach relationships and what they prioritize in a partner. However, by following universal principles such as open communication, mutual respect, and a commitment to personal growth, individuals and couples can find and sustain love, regardless of their differences.

6. Intimacy problems

Introduction:

Love relationships give us the opportunity to experience intimacy with others emotionally, physically, and even spiritually. A significant aspect of a successful relationship is the ability to establish intimacy that is emotionally rewarding, consistent, and fulfilling. However, not all relationships experience this kind of intimacy, and this can lead to problems; this paper explores the common intimacy problems that affect relationships and how one can find and sustain love amidst them.

Common Intimacy Problems in Relationships:

Low Emotional Intimacy:

Emotional intimacy is the primary form of intimacy in any relationship. Unfortunately, this kind of intimacy can be one of the most challenging to achieve. Being emotionally intimate is daunting for some people, and this can interfere with the development of a relationship. Avoiding emotional intimacy can be due to shame, fear of vulnerability or rejection, or poor communication skills. Low emotional intimacy can leave a relationship feeling hollow or empty.

One way to increase emotional intimacy is by being open and honest with one another. However, this can only happen if both partners communicate effectively with one another. By sharing one's thoughts and feelings, one can strengthen the emotional bond with their partner and create a positive and comfortable environment in the relationship.

Lack of Physical Intimacy:

Physical intimacy is also crucial in any romantic relationship. However, it's not just about sexual activities; it also involves cuddling, hugging, kissing, and expressing affection through touch. Notably, physical intimacy contributes to happy and healthy relationships.

The lack of physical intimacy can be due to several reasons, including physical distance, health problems, communication barriers, or a lack of interest in sexual activities. This problem requires open and honest communication to find out the underlying cause and how to address it.

Infidelity:

Infidelity poses a severe threat to any romantic relationship. Once trust is broken by one of the partners, it can be challenging to rebuild the relationship. Infidelity can occur due to a lack of emotional or physical intimacy in the relationship. Cheating is a risky decision that often leads to more heartache than the initial issue in the relationship.

Overcoming the effects of infidelity requires transparency, open communication, and forgiveness by both parties. It may take a long time to regain trust, emotional intimacy, and a healthy relationship.

Issues Related to Communication:

Poor communication is another leading cause of intimacy problems in relationships. Couples who cannot communicate effectively often end up with misunderstandings and unresolved conflicts. Avoiding or miscommunicating during important conversations can lead to a breakdown in intimacy.

One way to improve communication is to set aside dedicated time to talk to one another, without distractions. Additionally, active listening, maintaining eye contact, and asking open-ended questions can improve communication. A therapist may also assist with providing tools and techniques to facilitate effective communication.

Difficulty in Trusting Others:

Trust is a fundamental factor in any relationship. However, mistrust can lead to many intimacy problems. For example, a partner may be unwilling to share their thoughts and feelings with someone they don't trust, leading to a lack of emotional intimacy.

Allowing oneself to trust others is a vulnerable decision. It involves taking risks, being open to new experiences, and letting go of personal insecurities or past experiences. It takes time to develop trust, but it can be achieved by being patient, being honest, and choosing to have faith in one's partner.

How to Find and Sustain Love:

Although there are intimacy problems in relationships, one can still find and sustain love by implementing the following tips:

Be Yourself:

It's important to be true to oneself and be comfortable with who you are. When one is genuine, they attract like-minded individuals who respect and appreciate them for who they are. When one attempts to hold back or change their personality, they will likely end up in a relationship that does not meet their needs, leading to intimacy problems.

Communicate Effectively:

Effective communication involves listening, being honest, and being open-minded. When one's partner feels heard, they can reciprocate by listening as well. Effective communication is key to building intimacy and avoiding conflicts.

Establish Shared Values:

Shared values and interests are crucial in any intimate relationship. When one shares similar values, they are more likely to build a strong bond. Additionally, sharing similar interests or activities can foster feelings of connection and mutual respect.

Work towards Personal Growth:

Personal development and growth are essential in any healthy relationship. A partner who is continually working on self-esteem, communication skills, and setting personal goals is likely to establish successful relationships. Personal growth is a never-ending process; it's a commitment to being the best version of oneself.

Be Honest and Transparent:

Honesty and transparency are crucial in any relationship, to create trust and intimacy. A partner who is honest is likely to establish more profound connections with their partner.

Conclusion:

Intimacy problems are significant contributors to relationship breakdowns. However, with effective communication, honesty, mutual respect, and understanding, couples can work towards building long-lasting, healthy, and loving relationships. It's essential to do the necessary work to achieve lasting and fulfilling relationships. By being oneself, communications effectively, working towards personal growth, and establishing shared values, it's possible to find and sustain love.

7. Lack of emotional support

Introduction

Love is a basic human need, and it is essential for our emotional and psychological well-being. According to Maslow's hierarchy of needs, love and belongingness come after physiological and safety needs. Therefore, people seek love and a sense of belongingness to fulfill their emotional needs. However, the journey to finding and sustaining love can be challenging, especially when one lacks emotional support. Emotional support is the provision of comfort and care to someone in need, and it is crucial in relationships. The lack of emotional support not only affects one's life but also affects their ability to establish and maintain a healthy relationship. This paper examines the effects of the lack of emotional support in finding and sustaining love and provides solutions to overcome this challenge.

Effects of the Lack of Emotional Support on Finding Love

1. Low Self-esteem and Confidence

People who lack emotional support may develop low self-esteem and self-confidence, which can affect their ability to find love. Low self-esteem and self-confidence can cause people to feel insecure, unlovable, and unworthy of love. People who lack emotional support may have a hard time building relationships because they feel like they are not good enough for their partners. Additionally, low self-esteem can make people overly dependent on their partners, leading to the development of toxic relationships.

2. Fear of Vulnerability

In a healthy relationship, there is a need for vulnerability, which helps to build intimacy and trust. Vulnerability involves opening up and sharing one's emotions, thoughts, and feelings with their partners. However, people who lack emotional support may find it challenging to be vulnerable with their partners. They may have developed a fear of vulnerability due to past experiences of rejection, abandonment, or neglect. Consequently, fear of vulnerability can prevent people from finding love because they are not willing to be open and honest about their feelings.

3. Difficulty Establishing Boundaries

Effective communication and establishing boundaries are critical in healthy relationships. However, people who lack emotional support may have difficulty establishing and communicating boundaries with their partners. They may be afraid of losing their partners if they set boundaries or communicate their needs and desires. Moreover, they may not even be aware of their boundaries because they have not had the opportunity to develop them.

4. Attracted to Unhealthy Relationships

People who lack emotional support may be drawn to unhealthy relationships because they are familiar with dysfunction and chaos. They may have grown accustomed to neglect, abuse, or codependency, leading them to seek similar relationships. This can be attributed to the fact that people tend to recreate familiar patterns of behavior. As a result, people who lack emotional support may not know how to establish healthy relationships, and this can affect their ability to find and sustain love.

Effects of the Lack of Emotional Support on Sustaining Love

1. Lack of Intimacy

Intimacy involves emotional closeness, trust, and vulnerability. It is an essential aspect of a healthy relationship. However, people who lack emotional support may have difficulties being intimate because they have not developed emotional closeness and trust. Additionally, they may find it challenging to express themselves emotionally, leading to a lack of intimacy in their relationships.

2. Emotional Withdrawal

Emotional withdrawal involves withholding emotions and feelings from one's partner. Emotional withdrawal can develop due to the fear of vulnerability or intimacy. People who lack emotional support may find it challenging to share their emotions with their partners, leading to emotional withdrawal. Emotional withdrawal can cause the breakdown of relationships, leading to a lack of sustainment of love.

3. Inability to Communicate

Communication is a critical aspect of relationships. Effective communication involves expressing emotions, thoughts, and feelings to one's partner. However, people who lack emotional support may have difficulty communicating their needs and desires to their partners. They may not know how to express themselves emotionally, leading to a breakdown in communication and a lack of sustainment of love.

4. Dependence on the Relationship

People who lack emotional support may become overly dependent on their relationships because they view them as their source of emotional support. This can lead to a lack of autonomy, self-esteem, and confidence. Additionally, it can cause people to prioritize their relationships over their well-being, leading to neglect of self-care.

Solutions to Overcome the Lack of Emotional Support in Finding and Sustaining Love

1. Seek Therapy

People who lack emotional support can benefit from therapy. Therapy provides a safe and supportive environment where individuals can explore their emotions and past experiences. Therapy can help individuals develop healthy coping mechanisms and communicate effectively.

2. Develop Boundaries and Effective Communication

Developing boundaries and effective communication is crucial for healthy relationships. It is essential to communicate one's needs and desires explicitly to prevent misunderstandings and conflicts. Additionally, setting boundaries helps to establish a healthy balance between one's relationships and personal life.

3. Focus on Self-Care

Focusing on self-care is crucial in overcoming the lack of emotional support. Self-care involves taking care of oneself physically, mentally, and emotionally. This helps to develop self-esteem, self-confidence, and autonomy. Additionally, focusing on self-care helps to prevent emotional dependence on relationships.

4. Practice Vulnerability

Practicing vulnerability involves being open and honest about one's emotions, thoughts, and feelings. Being vulnerable can help to establish intimacy and trust in relationships. Additionally, being vulnerable can help individuals overcome their fear of vulnerability and help them find and sustain love.

Conclusion

Love is an essential human need, and the lack of emotional support can affect one's ability to find and sustain love. The lack of emotional support can lead to low self-esteem and self-confidence, fear of vulnerability, difficulty establishing boundaries, and attraction to unhealthy relationships. Additionally, the lack of emotional support can result in a lack of intimacy, emotional withdrawal, inability to communicate, and dependence on relationships. To overcome the lack of emotional support, individuals should seek therapy, develop boundaries and effective communication, focus on self-care, and practice vulnerability. By focusing on these solutions, individuals can overcome their lack of emotional support and find and sustain healthy relationships.

8. Codependency issues

Introduction

Being in a romantic relationship can be a fulfilling experience, especially when one shares love with a significant other. However, maintaining a healthy and long-lasting relationship requires effort and dedication from both partners. Many people struggle to sustain love in their relationships due to codependency issues. Codependency is a behavioral problem that arises when one partner depends on another partner excessively to meet their emotional and psychological needs. In this essay, we will discuss the symptoms, causes, and solutions of codependency in relationships and how to find and sustain love.

Definition of Codependency

Codependency is a behavioral condition where a person relies on their partner excessively to cater to their physical and emotional needs. It is characterized by an unhealthy attachment, where one party enables the other partner to continue with self-destructive patterns. According to Melody Beattie, the author of "Codependent No More," codependency is a learned behavior that can develop from various factors, including family upbringing, emotional abuse, and neglect. Codependent individuals often have a low sense of self-worth and self-esteem, which drives them to seek validation from their partner continually. They often have trouble setting boundaries, saying "no" to their partner, and are quick to feel guilty when they do not meet their partner's needs.

Symptoms of Codependency

Codependency can manifest in various ways in relationships. Some of the common symptoms of codependency include:

1. Need for Validation: Codependent individuals often rely on their partner to affirm their self-worth and self-esteem. They require excessive attention, flattery, and appreciation from their partner, and feel lost without it.

2. Low Self-Esteem: They often have a negative self-image, lack confidence, and feel inadequate in most situations.

3. Control Issues: Codependent individuals tend to have control issues where they try to control their partner's thoughts, actions, and emotions to satisfy their needs.

4. Over-Sensitivity: Codependent people are often oversensitive to their partner's feelings and emotions. They tend to take everything personally, get defensive, and feel overly responsible for their partner's happiness.

5. Poor Boundaries: Codependent individuals often have trouble setting boundaries, saying "no" to their partner, and are quick to feel guilty when they do not meet their partner's needs.

Causes of Codependency

Codependency can stem from various factors, including family upbringing, past trauma, and societal pressures. The following are some of the causes of codependency.

1. Family Upbringing: Codependency can develop from a family dynamic in which parents or siblings had substance abuse, emotional issues, or mental illness. Children in such environments often adopt a caretaker role and neglect their own needs.

2. Past Trauma: Individuals who experienced physical, emotional, or sexual abuse in their past can develop codependency as a way of coping with the trauma.

3. Societal Pressures: Societal norms and expectations can also lead to codependency. Some people may feel pressure to conform to certain social expectations, such as getting married or having children, leading them to seek validation from their partners to meet these expectations.

Solutions to Codependency

Codependency can be a significant challenge in any relationship, but it can be overcome through various solutions. The following are some of the solutions to codependency in relationships.

1. Self-Love: Codependent individuals need to prioritize self-love and self-care. It involves developing a positive self-image, practicing self-compassion, and learning to meet their own needs.

2. Communication: Open and honest communication is key in overcoming codependency. It involves expressing one's feelings and emotions to their partner, setting boundaries, and learning to say "no."

3. Therapy: Therapy is an effective way of addressing codependency issues. It provides a safe space to explore past traumas, identify unhealthy patterns, and develop strategies to overcome them.

4. Mindfulness Practices: Mindfulness practices, such as meditation, yoga, and deep breathing, can help individuals develop self-awareness, reduce stress, and improve mental health.

How to Find and Sustain Love

Finding and sustaining love can be challenging, especially for individuals struggling with codependency. The following are some of the tips for finding and sustaining love.

1. Know Yourself: It is essential to know oneself and what one wants in a relationship. This involves identifying one's values, goals, preferences, and boundaries.

2. Practice Self-Love: Self-love and self-care are essential in any relationship. It involves developing a positive self-image, practicing self-compassion, and learning to meet one's own needs.

3. Communication: Communication is essential in any relationship. It involves expressing one's feelings and emotions, setting boundaries, and learning to say "no."

4. Balance: A healthy relationship requires balance and mutual respect. Both partners should strive to meet each other's needs and desires while respecting each other's boundaries.

5. Patience: Building a long-lasting relationship takes time and patience. It involves investing time in getting to know each other, building trust, and establishing a strong foundation.

Conclusion

Codependency can be a significant challenge in any relationship, but it can be overcome through self-love, therapy, and communication.

When seeking love, it is essential to prioritize one's needs, values, and expectations, and communicate them clearly to potential partners. A healthy relationship requires balance, mutual respect, and understanding. It takes time, patience, and effort to build a strong and long-lasting relationship, but it is possible with the right mindset and strategies.

9. Quiz

1. What is one common issue that affects finding and sustaining love?

a) Insecurity
  b) Fear of rejection
  c) Lack of communication
  d) All of the above

2. What can help overcome insecurity and increase self-esteem?

a) Positive self-talk
  b) Self-care practices
  c) Seeking therapy or counseling
  d) All of the above

3. What is a common mistake people make when searching for love?

a) Setting unrealistic expectations
  b) Settling for less than what they deserve
  c) Overlooking important values and compatibility factors
  d) All of the above

4. What can help sustain love in a relationship?

a) Regular communication and openness
   b) Quality time and shared experiences
   c) Prioritizing the relationship
   d) All of the above

5. What often happens when couples neglect to communicate effectively?

a) They become distant and disconnected
   b) They start to argue and fight more frequently
   c) Misunderstandings and assumptions arise
   d) All of the above

Answers:
   1. d) All of the above
   2. d) All of the above
   3. d) All of the above
   4. d) All of the above
   5. d) All of the above

VI. Conclusion

1. Reflection on personal growth and relationship success

Introduction

Finding and sustaining love is one of the most important aspects of human life. Relationships help to shape our personal growth and development, and they provide a space for us to experience love, intimacy, and connection. However, building and maintaining a successful relationship requires effort, introspection, and self-awareness. In this essay, I reflect on my personal growth and relationship successes in relation to the book, "How to Find and Sustain Love" by Linda Carroll. I explore how the concepts in the book have impacted my relationships and personal growth journey.

Part One: Personal Growth

Personal growth is an ongoing process that involves cultivating self-awareness, acquiring new life skills, and developing a positive mindset. In the book, "How to Find and Sustain Love," Carroll emphasizes the importance of personal development in achieving successful relationships. This concept resonated with me because I have experienced how my personal growth has positively influenced my relationships.

One of the most significant areas of my personal growth journey has been my emotional intelligence. Emotional intelligence refers to the ability to identify, understand, and manage one's emotions and the emotions of others. Carroll emphasizes the importance of emotional intelligence in building strong and healthy relationships. In my experience, emotional intelligence has been crucial in helping me navigate conflicts and communicate effectively with my partner.

Another area of personal growth that I have worked on is my self-esteem. Self-esteem refers to our inner sense of worth and value. In the book, Carroll emphasizes that a lack of self-esteem can lead to relationship problems such as jealousy and insecurity. Through therapy and self-reflection, I have worked on building my self-esteem, which has helped me to recognize and address any negative thought patterns that may impact my relationships.

Finally, the book also emphasizes the importance of maintaining a positive mindset and engaging in self-care. Carroll suggests that a positive mindset and self-care practices can help people attract and sustain loving relationships. In my personal growth journey, I have found that mindfulness practices such as meditation and gratitude journaling have helped me maintain a positive mindset and reduce stress.

Part Two: Relationship Success

Relationship success involves building and maintaining strong, healthy, and fulfilling relationships. In "How to Find and Sustain Love," Carroll explores the elements that contribute to successful relationships. These elements include communication, trust, shared values, and emotional intimacy.

Communication is one of the most critical elements of successful relationships. In the book, Carroll emphasizes the importance of communication in building trust, resolving conflicts, and maintaining emotional intimacy. Communication has been a significant challenge for me in my past relationships. Through therapy and personal reflection, I have developed better communication skills, including active listening and expressing my needs and feelings more effectively.

Trust is another essential element of successful relationships. Carroll suggests that building trust requires honesty, consistency, and open communication. I have found that being truthful with my partner, even when it is difficult, has helped us build a foundation of trust. Additionally, being consistent in my actions and words has also helped to strengthen our trust in each other.

Shared values are also crucial in successful relationships. Carroll emphasizes the importance of being with someone whose values align with our own. I have found that having shared values with my partner has helped us to navigate conflicts and make decisions together more effectively.

Finally, emotional intimacy is a critical component of successful relationships. Emotional intimacy refers to the ability to share our deepest thoughts and feelings with our partners. In the book, Carroll suggests that emotional intimacy requires vulnerability and courage.

For me, building emotional intimacy has required me to be more open and vulnerable with my partner, even when it is uncomfortable.

Conclusion

In conclusion, finding and sustaining love requires personal growth and development. In "How to Find and Sustain Love," Carroll explores the concepts that contribute to successful relationships, including emotional intelligence, self-esteem, trust, communication, shared values, and emotional intimacy. Through my personal growth journey, I have found that the concepts in this book have helped me to build stronger, healthier, and more fulfilling relationships. By continuing to work on my personal growth and development, I can continue to build successful relationships and experience the love, connection, and intimacy that we all desire.

2. Encouragement to continue practicing healthy relationship habits

Introduction

Healthy relationships are an essential aspect of living a fulfilling life. They can be the source of joy, support, and happiness. However, as anyone who has ever been in a relationship will know, it takes more than just love to maintain a healthy and happy relationship.

It takes work, commitment, and constant effort to keep a relationship strong and successful. Just like any other skill, maintaining healthy relationships requires practice and repetition to become a habit. This paper seeks to encourage individuals to continue practicing healthy relationship habits for long-lasting and sustaining love.

Communication

Communication is a vital aspect of any healthy relationship. Without it, individuals cannot express their feelings, thoughts, or needs, which can lead to misunderstandings and conflicts. Therefore, it is paramount to encourage individuals to practice healthy communication habits.

One way to strengthen communication skills is by regularly checking in with one's partner. Checking in can be as simple as asking them how their day was, their feelings about a particular issue, or how they are feeling. This not only keeps the lines of communication open but also ensures that both individuals are on the same page concerning their relationship.

Another important communication habit to cultivate is active listening. Active listening involves giving your partner your undivided attention without interrupting or dismissing their feelings. By actively listening, individuals can better understand their partner's perspective, feelings, and needs, which fosters empathy, trust, and mutual respect.

Moreover, nonverbal communication can also have a significant impact on a relationship. Good body language, such as eye contact, can show that one is present and attentive to their partner. Facial expressions, touch, and tone of voice can also convey emotions, intentions, and attitudes towards your partner. Therefore, individuals must practice healthy non-verbal communication habits as well.

Trust

Trust is another essential aspect of a healthy relationship. It enables individuals to feel safe, respected, and supported in their relationship. Therefore, it is imperative to encourage individuals to practice healthy trust habits.

One way to cultivate trust is by being honest and transparent with one's partner. Honesty creates a foundation of openness and accountability in the relationship, which builds trust and mutual respect. Sharing vulnerabilities and being truthful about mistakes and challenges in the relationship can also foster deeper emotional connections and a stronger relationship.

Another essential aspect of trust is keeping commitments. Following through on promises, agreements, and commitments, no matter how small, demonstrates reliability and dependability, which builds trust in the relationship. This requires individuals to be accountable for their actions and communicate effectively when plans or commitments cannot be fulfilled.

Finally, it is important to avoid behaviors that erode trust, such as dishonesty, cheating, and concealing information. Trust can take a long time to build, but it can be quickly lost with such behaviors. Therefore, individuals must cultivate healthy habits in their relationship to build and maintain trust.

Respect

Respect is an essential ingredient in a healthy relationship. It is about treating one's partner with dignity, kindness, and consideration. Practicing healthy respect habits is essential for long-lasting and sustainable love.

One way to respect one's partner is by valuing their opinions, beliefs, and feelings. Listening to their perspective without criticism or judgment and acknowledging their thoughts and feelings shows that one respects their partner's agency and autonomy in the relationship.

Another crucial aspect of respect is finding ways to support one's partner's dreams, goals, and aspirations. Supporting a partner's endeavors, no matter how big or small, can foster mutual respect, understanding, and a sense of togetherness. Celebrating each other's successes is also an excellent way to show appreciation and recognition for your partner's achievements.

Finally, respect also means setting healthy boundaries in the relationship. Boundaries are essential for maintaining individuality, personal space, and self-care. It shows that one respects each other's autonomy and values, leading to more secure and sustainable love.

Intimacy

Intimacy is an essential aspect of a healthy relationship. It can take various forms, such as physical, emotional, or spiritual intimacy. Practicing healthy intimacy habits strengthens the bond between individuals in a relationship.

One effective way of cultivating intimacy is by consistently showing affection to one's partner. Physical touch, such as holding hands, hugging, and kissing, can create feelings of warmth, comfort, and security. It also communicates to the partner that they are valued and loved.

Another way to cultivate intimacy is by consistently demonstrating emotional support. This means regularly expressing love, appreciation, and gratitude towards one's partner. It also involves being present and supportive emotionally when one's partner is in need.

Finally, spiritual intimacy can also contribute positively to a relationship. Partner's who share spiritual values or beliefs can foster a deeper sense of meaning and purpose in their relationship. They can also cultivate a sense of shared connection and trust, enabling long-lasting and sustainable love.

Self-improvement

Self-improvement is an essential aspect of maintaining a healthy and sustainable relationship. It involves cultivatin healthy personal habits that can help build a better relationship.

One important personal habit is self-care. Self-care involves taking care of one's physical, emotional, and mental wellbeing. It involves healthy eating, regular exercise, meditation, and getting enough rest. Cultivating self-care routines means one's partner is free from the burden of taking care of their wellbeing alone, leading to a happier and more sustainable relationship.

Another personal habit is being supportive of one's partner's self-improvement. This means encouraging them to pursue their interests, aspirations, and dreams. Supporting their personal growth can provide a sense of emotional fulfillment, leading to a more adept and fulfilling romantic relationship.

Conclusion

In conclusion, practicing healthy relationship habits is essential for finding and sustaining love. Communication, trust, respect, intimacy, and self-improvement are essential aspects of maintaining a healthy and sustainable relationship. Cultivating these habits takes practice, commitment, and effort. Encouraging individuals to practice healthy relationship habits can lead to long-lasting and fulfilling romantic relationships.

3. Quiz

1. Which of the following is NOT a key aspect to finding and sustaining love?

    A) Communication
    B) Trust
    C) Financial stability
    D) Respect

2. Why is it important to have realistic expectations in a relationship?

    A) It is easier to maintain a positive attitude when expectations are not too high
    B) Unrealistic expectations can lead to disappointment and frustration
    C) Realistic expectations can lead to a deeper connection between partners
    D) All of the above

3. What is one way to overcome trust issues in a relationship?

    A) Be honest and transparent with your partner
    B) Keep secrets to yourself to avoid causing any issues
    C) Avoid confrontation and hope the issue eventually goes away
    D) None of the above

4. Why is it important to prioritize both individual and shared interests in a relationship?

    A) To avoid boredom and lack of excitement in the relationship
    B) To ensure that each partner feels valued and respected

C) To cultivate a sense of independence in each partner

D) All of the above

5. What role does forgiveness play in sustaining love?

A) It allows partners to move past any mistakes or conflicts

B) It builds trust and emotional closeness between partners

C) It cultivates a sense of empathy and compassion in the relationship

D) All of the above

Answers:

1. C) Financial stability

2. B) Unrealistic expectations can lead to disappointment and frustration

3. A) Be honest and transparent with your partner

4. D) All of the above

5. D) All of the above